Maunsell Moguls

Maunsell Moguls

Peter Swift

Ian Allan
PUBLISHING

Front cover, top: Maunsell 'N'-class No 31868, of Redhill (75B) shed, calls at North Camp station, with a Reading–Redhill service in July 1963. *T. B. Owen / Colour-Rail*

Front cover, bottom: Virginia Water, junction of the Reading and Weybridge lines to Waterloo via Richmond, is the location for 'U'-class 2-6-0 No 31625, in charge of a mixed goods bound for Feltham yard on 23 June 1957. *T. B. Owen / Colour-Rail*

Back cover, top: Athenry, in County Galway, is the location of this shot of Class K1a No 396 on 26 June 1951. This locomotive remained in traffic until October 1959. *W. A. Camwell / Stephenson Locomotive Society*

Back cover, bottom: Rebuilt 'River' class No 1790 is seen at Yeovil shed on 9th June 1935. *Stephenson Locomotive Society*

Previous page: 'U' class No 31624 leaving Southampton Central on a train for Andover and the Midland & South Western Junction line in January 1954. The three GWR carriages, of three generations, are in carmine and cream livery. *Colour-Rail (BRS412)*

Above: On 10 April 1953 a Victoria–Ramsgate–Birchington express is seen leaving Broadstairs behind 'N' class No 31854. *W. A. Corkill*

First published 2012

ISBN 978 0 7110 3400 6

Published by Ian Allan Publishing

an imprint of Ian Allan Publishing Ltd, Hersham, Surrey, KT12 4RG.

Printed in Malta.

Distributed in the United States of America and Canada by BookMasters Distribution Services.

Visit the Ian Allan Publishing website at www.ianallanpublishing.com

Contents

Acknowledgements

This book deals with a family of 204 locomotives which were derived from a single basic design. All used the same boiler and had many other features in common. There were 2-6-0 tender and 2-6-4 tank variants with either two or three cylinders and with 5ft 6in or 6ft driving wheels. All possible permutations of these variations were used, not all on the Southern. During their time, they operated under eight railway administrations whilst some had been purchased by a ninth company, which had been taken over before they could be put into service. The type operated all forms of traffic from express passenger and heavy freight to branch line services, and five survive on heritage railways.

The purpose of this book is to provide modellers with information on the changes which occurred to the external appearance of the Maunsell Mogul family of locomotives over the years.

Numerous books and articles have been published describing various aspects of the Moguls; those which have been of most use in preparing the text for this book are listed in the Bibliography, in the order of publication.

For the provision of photographs, I have used mainly my own collection and the Ian Allan photographic archive, including the Stephenson Locomotive Society collection, to which Nick Grant provided free access. I am aware that not every variety of locomotive has been covered, there are too many of them. I am indebted to all those photographers whose material has found its way into my own collection over many years, in many cases with no record of the source of the photograph. Both my own and the Ian Allan collections include H. C. Casserley prints, courtesy of Richard Casserley, and my collection includes prints from Rod Blencowe's collection and the Ted West collection, supplied by Mike King of the South Western Circle. John Harvey and Ken Rogers have kindly supplied scans from their collection to fill some gaps. As ever, colour slides from the Colour-Rail collection have been made available to the publisher.

For putting me right on details, I am most grateful to those two long-time students of Southern Railway locomotives, Eric Youldon and John Harvey. Both of these gentlemen looked through my draft texts and suggested many amendments, additions and corrections. As the Maunsell Moguls were overhauled at Ashford, until their very last years, we do not have the benefit of the records of George Woodward of Eastleigh and I have not attempted to record every change to every locomotive. Bob Allen of the Mid-Hants Railway provided useful information on the boilers and tenders of the three Mid-Hants Moguls.

Using the contacts available through the Historical Model Railway Society, I am most grateful to Alan O'Rourke and Leslie Bevis-Smith, the Irish Broad Gauge and Metropolitan stewards of the HMRS, for reading and commenting on my draft texts on 'their' versions of the Maunsell Moguls. Alan drew my attention to two very useful articles published in the Journal of the Irish Railway Record Society.

Peter H. Swift, Spondon, Derby, April 2012

Recommended reading:
R. N. Clements, *The Woolwich Locomotives of CIE*, IRRS, 1958
D. L. Bradley, *Locomotives of the SE&CR*, RCTS, 1961
H. Holcroft, *Locomotive Adventure Volume 1*, Ian Allan, 1962
E. J. S. Gadsden, *Metropolitan Steam*, Roundhouse, 1963
H. Holcroft, *Locomotive Adventure Volume 2*, Ian Allan, 1965
D. Murray, *Woolwich Memories*, IRRS, 1969
L. Tavender, *Livery Register No 3 LSWR and Southern*, HMRS, 1970
J. W. P. Rowledge, *The Maunsell Moguls*, Oakwood, 1976
RCTS, *Locomotives of the LNER Part 9a: Classes L1 to N19*, RCTS, 1977
D. L. Bradley, *Locomotives of the SE&CR (Revised)*, RCTS, 1980
L. Elsey, *Profile of the Southern Moguls,* OPC, 1986
F. Goudie, *Metropolitan Steam Locomotives*, Capital Transport, 1990
J. E. Chacksfield, *Richard Maunsell: An Engineering Biography*, Oakwood, 1998

Introduction

The first Maunsell Mogul locomotives were a freight 2-6-0 and a passenger 2-6-4T for the South Eastern & Chatham Railway but they were developed into a family of related locomotives in Southern Railway days, with others in Ireland and on London's Metropolitan Railway.

The prime aim of this series of books is to provide modellers with information on the appearance of the locomotives at each period of their history. To this end, photographs of as many of the variants as possible, and covering as many of the livery variants as possible, are included, together with scale drawings.

The Maunsell Mogul family of locomotives was initiated on the railways of the South Eastern & Chatham Railways managing committee with two prototypes, a 2-6-4T of Class K for express passenger service and a 2-6-0 of Class N for freight service, built in 1917. These were followed by a further 14 of Class N and two more prototypes (with three cylinders) of Classes N1 and K1. The last three 'Ns' and the two three-cylinder locomotives were completed after the SE&CR had become the eastern section of the Southern Railway in 1923.

In 1919, construction of a further 100 2-6-0s to the 'N' class design was started at Woolwich Arsenal, as a government scheme to reduce unemployment in the armaments industry after the end of World War 1. Initially, none of the British railway companies was interested in buying any of these locomotives but, after the price was reduced, 27 sets of parts were purchased by Irish railways and were built up into 26 locomotives for the Irish 5ft 3in (1.6 metres) gauge and six sets of parts were purchased by the Metropolitan Railway and built as 2-6-4Ts. The Southern Railway purchased 50 more or less complete locomotives and most of the remaining components.

In 1925-6, the Southern built 19 more 'K' class 2-6-4Ts but, following a serious derailment, the 20 'Ks' and the single 'K1', a 2-6-4T, were rebuilt in 1928 as 2-6-0s of Classes U and U1. The Southern then built a further 30 'Us' and 20 'U1s'. In 1930-34, the Southern built five more three-cylinder 2-6-0s of Class N1 and fifteen more two-cylinder 2-6-0s of Class N. The final additions to the family were 15 three-cylinder 2-6-4Ts of Class W, for freight work in the London area, in 1932-6.

The two tables on pages 9 and 10 summarise the various locomotive classes within the Maunsell Mogul family. A total of 204 locomotives of 10 classes were built or rebuilt, using two wheel arrangements, two driving wheel diameters and two or three cylinders. The second table lists major dimensional variations of the different classes and is aimed particularly to help modellers who might wish to convert a model of one type of Mogul into one of the other varieties. The coupled wheelbase of those designed as tank locomotives was shorter than those designed to run with tenders, the width over cylinders was less for the three-cylinder than the two-cylinder locomotives and boiler pitch was 3in (76mm) more for locomotives with 6ft (1.83m) wheels than those with 5ft 6in (1.68m) wheels. An extra 3in (76mm) was added to the boiler pitch for three-cylinder types. Due to the wider track gauge, the Irish-built Moguls were 6½in (165mm) wider over platform and cylinders than those on the Southern, although the cab and tender bodies remained the same width.

Above: No 31858 leaves Deepdene with the 11.05 Reading–Redhill service on 2 January 1965. The 'N' class Moguls could be seen at the east and west extremities of the Southern. *G. D. King*

Below: 'N' class No 31860 leaving Dunmere Halt on the 12.25 Wadebridge–Bodmin North, 17 May 1962. The use of a Mogul on this service is unusual, an LMS Class 2 tank being the normal motive power at this time. This was one of the oldest sections of the Southern Railway, being opened by the Bodmin & Wadebridge Railway in 1834 and not being connected to the rest of the system until 1895. No 31860 retains Maunsell-type cylinders and chimney and is fitted with AWS. *S. C. Nash*

Above: 'U' class No 31802 shunting at Yeovil Pen Mill station, 6 September 1964. No 31802 has new frames and cylinders and a BR standard chimney. The conduit on the buffer beam shows AWS is fitted. The hanging front coupling shows why 'bash' plates were fitted to prevent damage to the AWS receiver. *G. T. Robinson*

Class	Wheel Arrgt	Driving Wheel Diameter	No of Cyls	Owners	Number Built	Dates to Service
K	2-6-4T	6ft 0in (1.83m)	2	SE&CR, SR	20 (to 'U')	1917-1926
K1	2-6-4T	6ft 0in (1.83m)	3	SR	1 (to 'U1')	1925
N	2-6-0	5ft 6in (1.68m)	2	SE&CR, SR, BR	80	1917-1934
N1	2-6-0	5ft 6in (1.68m)	3	SR, BR	6	1923-1930
U	2-6-0	6ft 0in (1.83m)	2	SR, BR	50	1928-1931
U1	2-6-0	6ft 0in (1.83m)	3	SR, BR	21	1928-1931
W	2-6-4T	5ft 6in (1.68m)	3	SR, BR	15	1932-1936
372	2-6-0	5ft 6in (1.68m)	2	MGWR, GSR, CIE	20	1925-1929
393	2-6-0	6ft 0in (1.83m)	2	GSR, CIE	6	1930
K	2-6-4T	5ft 6in (1.68m)	2	Met, LT, LNER, BR	6	1925

No 31834, banking on the 11.45 Waterloo–Ilfracombe on the final approach to Mortehoe, 8 August 1964. No 31834 has a Woolwich-built tender with square-ended buffer beams. Fire irons are all neatly stored. *Author's collection*

Class	Coupled Wheelbase	Width	Width over Platform	Width of Cab	Boiler Pitch
K	7ft 3in+7ft 9in (2.21m+2.36m)	8ft 10in (2.70m)	8ft 9in (2.67m)	8ft 4in (2.54m)	8ft 6in (2.59m)
K1	7ft 3in+7ft 9in (2.21m+2.36m)	8ft 5½in (2.32m)	8ft 9in (2.67m)	8ft 4in (2.54m)	8ft 9in (2.67m)
N	7ft 3in+8ft 3in (2.21m+2.52m)	8ft 10in (2.70m)	8ft 4in (2.54m)	7ft 7in (2.31m)	8ft 3in (2.52m)
N1	7ft 3in+8ft 3in (2.21m+2.52m)	8ft 5½in (2.32m)	8ft 4in (2.54m)	7ft 7in (2.31m)	8ft 6in (2.59m)
U	7ft 3in+7ft 9in (2.21m+2.36m)#	8ft 10in (2.70m)	8ft 10in (2.70m)*	8ft 4in (2.54m)*	8ft 6in (2.59m)
U	7ft 3in+7ft 9in (2.21m+2.36m)	8ft 10in (2.70m)	8ft 4in (2.54m)**	7ft 7in (2.31m)**	8ft 6in (2.59m)
U1	7ft 3in+7ft 9in (2.21m+2.36m)#	8ft 5½in (2.32m)	8ft 4in (2.54m)†	7ft 7in (2.31m)†	8ft 9in (2.67m)
W	7ft 3in+7ft 9in (2.21m+2.36m)	8ft 5½in (2.32m)	8ft 6½in (2.60m)	7ft 7in (2.31m)‡	8ft 6in (2.59m)
372	7ft 3in+8ft 3in (2.21m+2.52m)	9ft 4½in (2.86m)	8ft 10½in (2.71m)	7ft 7in (2.31m)	8ft 3in (2.52m)
393	7ft 3in+8ft 3in (2.21m+2.52m)	9ft 4½in (2.86m)	8ft 10½in (2.71m)	7ft 7in (2.31m)	8ft 6in (2.59m)
K	7ft 3in+8ft 3in (2.21m+2.52m)	8ft 9¾in (2.69m)	8ft 4in (2.54m)	8ft 3in (2.52m)	8ft 3in (2.52m)

*   'U' class Nos A790 to A809 retained the platform and cab widths of the 'K' class.
** 'U' class Nos A610 to A639 had the platform and cab width of the 'N' class.
†   'U1' No A890 initially kept its wide platform and cab width but was later narrowed.
‡   The cab and bunker of the 'W' class were 7ft 7in (2.31m) wide but the tanks were 8ft 4in (2.54m) wide.
#   'U' class Nos A790 to A809 and 'U1' class No A890 were 5in (127mm) longer from the rear coupled axle to the dragbox than the other 2-6-0s.

CHAPTER ONE

Origin of the Class

The origin of the Maunsell Moguls stemmed from a motive power crisis in the railways of Kent in the first decade of the 20th century. A new Chief Mechanical Engineer was appointed and brought together a team of outstanding locomotive engineers who had been involved with innovative locomotive design on other railways.

During the latter part of the 19th century, rail transport in the county of Kent had been provided by two companies, the South Eastern Railway (SER) and the London Chatham & Dover Railway (LCDR). They ran competing services to most of the major towns in the county. However, there was not enough traffic for two companies and the result was not only a poor return to the shareholders but also a lack of investment in improvements to the railways' infrastructure and a poor service to the people of Kent.

In 1898, the two companies finally decided that co-operation would be better than conflict and the South Eastern & Chatham Railways Managing Committee (SE&CR) was formed. This was not a full amalgamation, the two sets of shareholdings remaining separate until the formation of the Southern Railway in 1923, but for practical purposes, the SE&CR was now a single railway.

One obvious area where costs could be saved was the closure of the old LCDR Longhedge (Battersea) works, and transfer to the SER Ashford (Kent) works. Unfortunately, the transfer was not well managed and the SE&CR found itself with a severe shortage of usable locomotives at a time of increasing traffic. The Locomotive Carriage & Wagon Superintendent, H. S. Wainwright, took the blame and retired in November 1913 at the early age of 49. In selecting a successor, the SE&CR board were looking primarily for an able manager, and found one in the person of Richard Edward Lloyd Maunsell, Locomotive Superintendent of the Great

Southern & Western Railway (GS&WR) in Ireland. Maunsell was appointed Chief Mechanical Engineer to the SE&CR in November 1913.

Maunsell was born in County Dublin in 1868. He studied law at Trinity College, Dublin and concurrently became a pupil to H. A. Ivatt, Locomotive Superintendent of the GS&WR at Inchicore (Dublin). Having gained further experience on the Lancashire & Yorkshire and East Indian Railways, he returned to the GS&WR in 1896 as Assistant Locomotive Engineer and Works Manager, under the newly appointed Locomotive Superintendent, Robert Coey. When Coey retired in 1911, Maunsell was promoted to the top job at Inchicore. The only new locomotives built at Inchicore during his appointment were eight 0-6-0s and a single large 4-4-0, both of which were developments of designs prepared under Coey's chief draughtsman, Ernest Joynt.

On arrival at Ashford in December 1913, Maunsell's first priority was to sort out the mess in the works; his second priority was to provide new locomotives. Maunsell was primarily an engineering manager, not a locomotive designer. He knew what he wanted, locomotives which would move the traffic and would be easy to maintain, and he set about building up a team that could produce such locomotives.

Wainwright's Chief Draughtsman, Robert Surtees, was due to retire and was replaced by James Clayton, the assistant Chief Locomotive Draughtsman of the Midland Railway (MR) at Derby. Clayton had a wide experience

Above: In 1909, Harold Holcroft, an assistant to
G. J. Churchward of the GWR, made a study tour to the USA
and noted the use of Mogul-type locomotives by railways in
that country. On his return to Swindon, he designed a 2-6-0
using standard components from Churchward's
modernisation scheme for GWR motive power. The first was
built in 1911, No 4321 being the first of the second batch
built in 1913. *Ian Allan Library*

Below: The prototype Maunsell Mogul No 810, built at
Ashford in 1917. It combines the most advanced features of
the GWR '43xx' class 2-6-0 and the S&DJR 2-8-0, having a
high superheat taper boiler and long-travel valves driven by
outside Walschaerts valve gear. What appears to be a steam
dome is only a cover over the top feed. No 810 is in the plain
slate grey livery adopted by Maunsell on the SE&CR and,
in accordance with the requirements of the SE&CR's route
codes, has only four lamp brackets on the front.
Author's collection

Above: James Clayton, assistant Chief Locomotive Draughtsman with the Midland Railway at Derby, designed a 2-8-0 locomotive to work freight traffic over the Mendip hills on the Somerset & Dorset Joint Railway. Six were built in 1914. They were larger and more advanced than anything the Midland used on its own system, with outside mounted Walschaerts valve gear but with short-travel valves. A change of management at Derby blocked Clayton's expected promotion and he joined Maunsell's team as Chief Draughtsman at Ashford. *Ian Allan Library*

Below: No 790, the prototype Maunsell 'K' class 2-6-4T, built at Ashford in 1917. The locomotive has a lot in common with the unbuilt 2-6-4T which James Clayton had designed for the London Tilbury & Southend Railway after the Midland had taken that company over in 1912. Clayton's locomotive would not have had the taper boiler or long-travel valves. When new, both prototypes Nos 790 and 810 had mechanical lubricators mounted above the left-hand cylinder. *Author's collection*

of innovative engineering. After training with Beyer Peacock and as a draughtsman at Ashford, he worked in the newly developing motor industry, before being taken into the personal employment of Cecil Paget. Paget was Locomotive Works Manager at Derby and son of the Midland Chairman and was building, at his own cost, a 2-6-2 with four double-ended cylinders, sleeve valves and dry-sided firebox, 40 years before Bulleid's 'Leader'! When Paget's brainchild failed to come up to expectations, Clayton had moved into the drawing office at Derby. Here, he had been involved with the design of a 2-8-0 for the Somerset & Dorset Joint Railway (SDJR), and a 2-6-4T for the lines of the London Tilbury & Southend Railway (LTSR), which the Midland had taken over in 1912. Both designs had superheated boilers and outside cylinders with Walschaerts valve gear, which were just becoming standard practice on Britain's railways, although they had

been normal in continental Europe, also for some time on British locomotives built for export. Unfortunately, the locomotive running department of the MR did not see the need for such locomotives, preferring to order more inside cylinder 0-6-0s and 4-4-0s until the late 1920s. The 2-8-0s were limited to six for the SDJR, with five more in 1925. The 2-6-4Ts were not built at Derby until 1927. There would clearly be more innovative work for Clayton at Ashford than at Derby.

During the first decade of the 20th century, George Jackson Churchward had been developing a new range of standard locomotives for the Great Western Railway (GWR) at Swindon. These featured major advances in boiler design, the boiler and firebox being tapered to provide the maximum steam-raising capacity with the minimum weight. Superheated steam and long-travel piston valves were giving performance and fuel economy which were unknown on other railways at the time in Britain, although Churchward continued to use inside valve gear at a time when the advantages of outside gear were beginning to be accepted elsewhere. In 1912, Harold Holcroft, who had worked for Churchward on special projects, had prepared the specification for the '43xx' class 2-6-0s, completing the range of GWR standard locomotives. Henceforward, the requirement of the GWR locomotive department was to produce more of the same, rather than continued innovation. It was time for some of Churchward's team to move on. Holcroft moved to the SE&CR as Maunsell's personal assistant, and George Pearson, the Assistant Carriage Works Manager at Swindon, became Maunsell's Assistant Chief Mechanical Engineer and Works Manager.

Maunsell's team produced drawings for a 2-6-0 ('N' class) for freight work and a 2-6-4T ('K' class)

for express passenger work. The 2-6-4T was similar to the one designed, but not built, at Derby for the LTS lines and the 2-6-0 could almost be described as a cross between Holcroft's '43xx' 2-6-0 for the GWR and Clayton's 2-8-0 for the SDJR. Both had the taper boiler and long-travel piston valves of Swindon practice, but with outside Walschaerts valve gear. Superficial details, such as the cab and tender, were typical of current Midland practice. Due to World War 1, only a single prototype of each type was built in 1917, but 15 more 2-6-0s were built between 1920 and 1923. The numbers of both types were increased in Southern Railway days.

When the Southern Railway was formed in 1923, Robert Urie, Chief Mechanical Engineer of the London & South Western Railway (LSWR) had reached retirement age and Lawson Billinton, of the London Brighton & South Coast Railway (LBSCR) did not have the experience of Maunsell, who was therefore appointed to the post of Chief Mechanical Engineer of the Southern Railway. Rather than locating himself at one of the existing locomotive design offices, Maunsell and a small personal team, including Clayton and Holcroft, were based at the Southern Railway headquarters at Waterloo Station (London).

Below: 'U' class 2-6-0 No 1792, rebuilt from a 'River' class 2-6-4T at Eastleigh in July 1928, stands at the side of Yeovil Town shed during the mid 1930s. The lining on the green smoke deflectors is clearly visible. By the time of its withdrawal in September 1964 it had been rebuilt with replacement frames and carried a BR Standard Class 4-type chimney. *Stephenson Locomotive Society*

CHAPTER TWO

The 'N' Class

The 'N' class 2-6-0 was conceived as a heavy freight locomotive for the South Eastern & Chatham Railway. To alleviate post-World War 1 unemployment in the munitions industry, more of the type were built at the Woolwich Arsenal, most of which were purchased by the newly formed Southern Railway, also the Metropolitan Railway and by railways in Ireland.

The first of Maunsell's 'N' class 2-6-0s, No 810, was completed by the SE&CR's Ashford works in July 1917. The taper boiler, with top feed in the dome and the regulator in the smokebox taking its steam via an internal pipe from the top rear end of the boiler, followed Swindon practice. The superheater was designed by Maunsell's team for easy maintenance. The outside cylinders with piston valves on top, driven by Walschaerts valve gear, followed recent practice at Derby. The driver's position on the right followed SE&CR practice but the general use of the steam reverser (developed by James Stirling of the SER) was replaced by a handwheel and screw. The cab front was provided with four 'spectacles', elongated windows to either side of the firebox shoulders and subsidiary round ports above the firebox This followed Wainwright's practice with Belpaire boilers. Braking was by steam on the locomotive and vacuum on the tender.

Fifteen further 'N' class were ordered from Ashford works in November 1917. Construction was delayed by the war and Nos 811 to 821 entered traffic between June 1920 and October 1922, followed by Nos 823 to 825 in May to December 1923 after the Southern Railway (SR) had taken over the SE&CR. No 825 was completed in the new SR livery and numbered A825. To avoid unemployment in the greatly expanded armaments industry at the end of World War 1, the government proposed that armaments manufacturers should undertake railway work. This would both reduce unemployment in the armaments industry and would help the railways in overcoming the backlog of equipment replacement caused by the war. A number of privately owned armaments manufacturers, and the government-owned Woolwich Arsenal, briefly joined the existing British locomotive building industry. During the war, Maunsell had been one of the members of the Association of Railway Locomotive Engineers (ARLE) involved in the design of a range of standard locomotives for the British railway companies in Britain. Orders were placed with Woolwich Arsenal in November 1915 for 50 each of the 2-6-0 and 2-8-0 types on which most design progress had been made. As the design of neither ARLE type was complete, it was decided that Woolwich should build 100 of Maunsell's 'N' class 2-6-0 instead. Ashford supplied all the drawings for the 'N' class (re-drawn to Woolwich practice) and supplied a number of specimen components. It was appreciated that Woolwich Arsenal did not have the expertise to build boilers, so 110 were obtained from established locomotive builders. First delivery was to be in September 1920 at a price of £10,000 per locomotive.

Construction of the locomotives was delayed, prices rose and potential orders disappeared. The government requested the company George Cohen & Armstrong Disposals Corporation to dispose of 50 partly assembled locomotives and such components as existed for the other 50. The first sale was to the Midland Great Western Railway (MGWR) in Ireland, which ordered 12 'sets of parts' in March 1923 for £24,000. Further sets of parts were sold to the Irish Great Southern Railways (GSR) and to the Metropolitan Railway.

Above: No 814 was completed at Ashford in November 1920. It was one of the production batch of 15 'N' class (Nos 811 to 825) ordered by the SE&CR from the Ashford works. No 822 was completed as the prototype three-cylinder 'N1' and the last three were not completed until after the SR had taken over the company. In preparation for the introduction of six-disc headcodes by the Southern, two additional lamp brackets are fitted low down either side of the smokebox. *Ian Allan Library*

Below: No A868 was built at Woolwich Arsenal and completed at Ashford in July 1925; it is seen here at Canterbury West on 4 September that year. The final 15 Woolwich Moguls were allocated to the eastern section to join the 16 SE&CR examples. After the steaming problems encountered by the SE&CR, Woolwich reverted to the original narrow chimney, apparently with no ill effect. No A868 is painted in Maunsell's green passenger livery, although the eastern section generally regarded the 'Ns' as freight locomotives. *Ian Allan Library*

In June 1923, *Locomotive Magazine* contained a report that one of the complete locomotives had been seen on the SR, carrying the number A20, which was the lowest vacant number in the eastern section series at the time. In Harold Holcroft's memoirs, he refers to riding on A20 with a passenger train between Ashford and Ramsgate on 27 April 1928, probably a transcription error from 1923.

In April 1924, the Southern Railway agreed to purchase 20 complete locomotives for £79,600, followed by 20 for £79,000 on 8 October and 10 for £39,500 on 5 November. The average price was £3,962 per locomotive, compared with Ashford's £8,970, although work at Ashford to complete the locomotives added an average of £840 to the price of each. The Southern paid a further £11,950 in November 1925 for the remaining material at

Above: SR No A847 was built at Woolwich Arsenal and completed at Ashford in February 1925, the second locomotive of the second batch. It is painted in Maunsell Dark Green and the photograph suggests that this is possibly the first of the Moguls to be painted in this livery. The mechanical lubricator above the cylinder is a non-standard feature. A847 was allocated to the western section. *Ian Allan Library*

Below: The Southern Railway may not have been impressed by the workmanship of Woolwich Arsenal but that did not prevent it sending No A866 to the 1925 British Empire Exhibition at Wembley. The locomotive was photographed at Clapham Junction on 23 May 1925. The motion has been disconnected and the boiler handrails and smokebox brackets polished for the show. *H. C. Casserley*

Woolwich Arsenal, which was used in the later examples of the Maunsell Mogul family built by the SR. Many of the 50 locomotives purchased by the SR were incomplete, Ashford works having to spend three weeks or more on each. The first part-built locomotives and tenders were delivered to Ashford in May 1924, with the first 20 being completed between June and September 1924. The final 30 were finished between January and September 1925. The Woolwich-built 'N' class locomotives were identical to the original SE&CR type, although some modifications, which had been found necessary on the SE&CR design, were incorporated whilst the Woolwich-built 'Ns' were being completed at Ashford. These were numbered A826 to A875 and were generally referred to as the

'Woolworths'. Woolworth's 'Five and Ten Cent Stores' had spread from the US to most British towns by the 1920s.

In 1930, an order was placed with Ashford works for a further 15 'N' class locomotives. They were delivered between July 1932 and January 1934, with the numbers 1400 to 1414. Compared with the previous 'N' class locomotives, all were built with front footsteps, no cylinder tailrods or by-pass valves and 'U1'-pattern chimney, all features which the earlier locomotives received as modifications. They also had twin slidebars and were coupled to 4,000gal (18,184-litre) tenders. Nos 1407 to 1414 were built with the driver's position on the left and smoke deflector plates.

Below: 'N' class No 1404 was completed at Ashford in October 1932. Nos 1400 to 1406 were built with front footsteps, no piston tailrods, cylinder or by-pass valves, and double slidebars. The wider chimney was introduced with the 'N1' class and 4,000gal tenders. *Ian Allan Library*

Bottom: No 1412 was completed at Ashford in December 1933. Nos 1407 to 1414 were built with left hand drive and smoke deflectors. Note the horizontal grab rails at the bottom and rectangular hand holes at the bottom of the front edge. The smoke deflector plates are clearly lined green. *Ian Allan Library*

CHAPTER THREE

The 'K' and 'U' Classes

The South Eastern & Chatham Railway built the first of
the 'K' class 2-6-4Ts as express passenger locomotives.
More were built by the Southern Railway.
After a derailment, all were rebuilt as 2-6-0s with a tender.
Further locomotives were built in that form.

The first of Maunsell's 'K' class 2-6-4Ts, No 790, was completed by the SE&CR's Ashford works in July 1917. The boiler, cylinders and motion were identical to those of the 'N' class 2-6-0. The driving wheels were 6ft (1.83m) diameter, compared with 5ft 6in (1.68m) on the 2-6-0 and the coupled wheelbase was 7ft 3in+7ft 9in (2.21+2.36m), compared with 7ft 3in + 8ft 3in (2.21+2.52m) on the 2-6-0, due to the proximity of the rear bogie. Although the width over the cylinders was the same as on the 2-6-0, the platform and cab were wider, to incorporate the side tanks. As on the 'N' class, the cab front incorporated four spectacles. Each side tank held 620gal (28,185-litre) of water and there was a 760gal (3,455-litre) tank under the coal bunker. Water capacity of 2,000gal (9,092-litre) and coal capacity of 2½ tons (2,540kg) compared with 3,500gal (15,911 litre) and 5 tons (5,080kg) on the 2-6-0. The 2-6-4T weighed 82½ tons (83,824kg), compared with 59½ton (60,455kg) for the 2-6-0, with most of the extra weight carried by the bogie and the leading truck. The maximum axle weight was 18½ton (18,797kg), only 1ton (1,016kg) more than that of the 2-6-0, allowing the 2-6-4T to run over most of the ex-SER main lines.

Ten futher 'K' class 2-6-4Ts were ordered from Ashford works in June 1920. Boilers were ordered from the North British Locomotive Co and cylinders, frames and side tanks from Woolwich Arsenal, which was already building 'N' class 2-6-0s. Due to capacity problems at Ashford, the components for nine 2-6-4Ts were sent to

Armstrong Whitworth & Co at Newcastle, (another armaments manufacturer building locomotives), for assembly. The tenth set of parts was used for the prototype 'K1' class three-cylinder 2-6-4T. The nine locomotives were delivered in May and June 1925 and numbered A791 to A799. All were provided with steam brakes on the locomotives and both vacuum and Westinghouse brakes for the train, the Westinghouse pump being mounted on the right side of the smokebox. The boilers of these locomotives incorporated longer superheater elements and regulators in the dome, features which were not externally apparent. Bob Allen of the Mid-Hants Railway confirms that the boilers now fitted to all three of the Mid-Hants Moguls have the regulators in the dome. Steam sanding and double slidebars were fitted. The prototype locomotive, No A790, was also fitted with Westinghouse brake equipment in May 1925, and double slidebars appeared at about the same time. The Southern Railway had a policy of naming express locomotives and the 'K' class were given the names of rivers on the Southern system.

A further 10 'K' class were ordered from the ex-LBSCR Brighton works in May 1925. They were delivered in July to December 1926 as Nos A800 to A809 and were not fitted for working Westinghouse braked trains. A futher 20 'Ks' were ordered in March 1926 but, before construction had proceeded, external events caused a change of plan.

Above: The prototype 'K' class No 790 was completed at Ashford, July 1917. The locomotive is at Bricklayers Arms *circa* 1920. Lamp brackets are now fitted on either side of the smokebox. Two sets of footsteps on bars descending from the running plate are fitted. A single step gives access to the motion, and a double (with hand holds on the tank sides) to provide access to the water filler. *R. Blencowe / W. Dunning*

Below: 'N' class No 1406, in Southern unlined black, at Battersea, 29 August 1948. *T. B. Owen / Colour-Rail (97285)*

Above: No 790 is now Southern Railway No A790 but is unnamed and retains the SE&CR plate on the bunker, *circa* 1923 or 1924. Single slidebars are retained but a shorter chimney is fitted. The mechanical lubricator has been removed. The locomotive was named *River Avon* in 1925 and fitted with double slidebars and provision for working air-braked trains on the central section of the Southern. *Ian Allan Library*

Below: 'K' class No A793 *River Ouse* was built by Armstrong Whitworth & Co, Newcastle and completed in May 1925. Compared with No A790, double slidebars are fitted; also the locomotive is fitted to work both vacuum-braked and air-braked trains. *Rail Archive Stephenson*

Above : No A799 *River Test* was another of the Armstrong Whitworth built dual braked locomotives. This view shows the Westinghouse pump. *Stephenson Locomotive Society*

Below: 'U' class No 1634 at Bournemouth Central in 1936. It is just possible to detect the lined green livery on the smoke deflectors. *Colour-Rail (SR102)*

There had already been complaints of poor riding of the 'K' class locomotives. Much of this had been ascribed to poor track but some modifications to the suspension had also been carried out. On 24 August 1927, No A800 *River Cray* was working the 17.00 Cannon Street–Deal express. Whilst travelling at about 55mph between Dunton Green and Sevenoaks, Kent, the locomotive began rolling and the leading coupled wheels became derailed. A set of catch points then caused the locomotive to derail completely, hitting the left abutment of an overbridge and falling against the side of the cutting through which the train was passing. The bridge was built with a separate brick arch over each track and the leading carriages were severely damaged by impact with the bridge abutments. Thirteen passengers were killed and many more were injured.

The Inquiry into the accident concluded that the track was defective; much of the SER main line was still ballasted with shingle and drainage had not been able to deal with recent rain. However, it was also agreed that the 'K' class were prone to roll on poor track and a decision was taken to rebuild all as a 2-6-0 with tender. Trials carried out with A803 *River Itchen* and the 'K1' three-cylinder 2-6-4T A890 *River Frome* on the LNER near Huntingdon showed that there was no problem at over 80mph on good track. The 'K1' class did show a propensity to roll, although not dangerously, during similar tests on the western section of the Southern near Woking.

The 20 'K' class 2-6-4Ts were rebuilt between February and July 1928 as 2-6-0s, classified 'U'. All retained the same numbers but lost their names. All three locomotive works of the SR were involved, Nos A790-A796 being rebuilt at Eastleigh, Nos A797 to A800, A802 and A805 at Ashford and Nos A801, A803, A804 and A806 to A809 at Brighton. All were fitted with 3,500gal (15,911-litre) tenders, similar to those coupled to the 'N' class. The wide platforms and cabs of the 'K' class were retained, with splashers over the driving wheels.

The 20 further 'K' class 2-6-4Ts which had already been ordered were completed as 'U' class 2-6-0s, as were 10 ordered in March 1929. Nos A610-A619 were completed at Brighton works between June and December 1928, Nos A620-A629 at Ashford between November 1928 and December 1929, and Nos A630-A639 at Ashford between February and May 1931. All retained the shorter coupled wheelbase of the 'K' class but distance between the rear coupled axle and the rear of the frames was 5in (127mm) less than on the rebuilt 2-6-4Ts. The cab was shorter and the platform alongside the boiler was higher than on the rebuilt 2-6-4Ts, so the splashers were much smaller. Front footsteps with sheet steel backing replaced the perilous-looking stanchions alongside the motion. The narrow cab and platform of the 'N' class was retained but with the cab front 'spectacles' shaped around the firebox shoulder. The A890-A809 series retained the four 'spectacles' as on the 'K' class 2-6-4Ts.

Below right: 'U1' 2-6-0 No A900 is seen at Guildford on a Waterloo–Portsmouth train formed of ex-LSWR timber-bodied corridor carriages on 20 August 1932. *Ian Allan Library*

Above: No A796 *River Stour* was rebuilt as a nameless 'U' class 2-6-0 at Eastleigh, returning to service in July 1928, still with dual brake. It is at Victoria, carrying the headcode for an Eastbourne train. *Ian Allan Library*

Below: A left side view of No A796. Although the Westinghouse pump is not visible, the two brake pipes on the buffer beam show that it is still dual braked. The 'Rebuilt Rivers' retained the wide platform and cab of the 2-6-4Ts. The elongated front cab window is swung open and the subsidiary round one provided on the 'Ns' and Rivers is clearly seen. *Author's collection*

Above: No A611 was ordered from Brighton as a 2-6-4T to be named *River Blackwater*. However, it was completed in August 1928 as a 2-6-0. The platform and cab of the '600' series 'U' class were the same width as the 'N' class 2-6-0s. A new type of cab-front 'spectacle' was provided, shaped to fit the top of the firebox. The Brighton-built batch, Nos A610-A619, were fitted with curved sandbox filler pipes, as provided on the 2-6-4Ts. *Rail Archive Stephenson*

Below: The last batch of 'U' class Nos A630-A639 were ordered as 2-6-0s. These were identical to Nos A610-A629 but were coupled to 4,000gal tenders. The boiler had flat-topped domes. No A631 was completed at Ashford in March 1931. *Ian Allan Library*

CHAPTER FOUR

Three-cylinder Moguls

The majority of the 204 Maunsell Moguls built
were simple two-cylinder locomotives.
There were also 42 locomotives built with three cylinders,
as four classes of 2-6-0 and 2-6-4T.

One of Maunsell's assistants, Harold Holcroft, had previously been an assistant to G. J. Churchward on the GWR at Swindon. In 1909, he had produced a design for a mechanism to work the valve of the middle cylinder on a three-cylinder locomotive from the valve gears of the outside cylinders. This had not been taken up by the GWR, which used either two or four cylinders on its locomotives. Holcroft moved to the SE&CR as Maunsell's personal assistant in 1914 and was employed initially on reorganising the company's Ashford (Kent) works. During a bout of sickness, he drew up a design for a three cylinder 4-4-0 with his conjugated valve gear and showed this to Maunsell. The valve of each outside cylinder was worked by a conventional Walschaerts valve gear. Each valve rod was then connected to the short end of a 2:1 ratio off centre pivoted horizontal lever. The long ends of these levers were connected to the ends of a floating lever between the frames, the centre point of which drove to the valve spindle of the inside cylinder.

Holcroft was not alone in looking at conjugated valve gears for three-cylinder locomotives. A very similar system was used on the Prussian State Railways Class S10₂ 4-6-0 of 1914. In 1915, Nigel Gresley, Chief Mechanical Engineer of the Great Northern Railway (GNR) at Doncaster, had designed a system where the right-hand valve rod drove the long end of a 2:1 lever set across the front of the locomotive. At the left-hand end there was pivoted a 1:1 lever with its ends connected to the left-hand and centre valve rods.

Geometrically, it produced the same result as Holcroft's system but with five, instead of nine, pin joints. A conjugating system is only worth having if it is simpler than an additional inside valve gear. In 1918, Gresley built No 461, a prototype three-cylinder 2-8-0. He wanted to use his conjugated gear but could not align it with the three valves, which were not in the same plane. He therefore used two transverse rocking shafts, each set across half the width of the locomotive, connected by vertical levers at the outer ends to the left- hand and right-hand valve spindles, with levers at the inner ends working the inside valve. This was similar to the system used on the Prussian Railways 'G12₁'class 2-10-0 of 1915 and on the 'Saxon XVIIIH' 4-6-2 of 1917. The parallel thinking of locomotive engineers in countries which were at war with each other at the time is intriguing.

Following publication of a description of GNR No 461 in *The Engineer*, Holcroft made some suggestions for improvements which led to a meeting between Holcroft and Gresley. Holcroft's suggestions enabled Gresley to use his preferred 2:1 lever system on all his larger locomotives built for GNR and the London & North Eastern Railway (LNER) after 1923. A further outcome of this meeting was that Gresley invited Holcroft to join him at Doncaster, a suggestion which was firmly vetoed by Maunsell who wished to use Holcroft's expertise to build three-cylinder locomotives for the Southern. A three-cylinder locomotive has three clear advantages over a two-cylinder machine.

Above: The prototype 'N1' class was completed at Ashford in March 1923. It is fitted with Gresley/Holcroft conjugated valve gear for the inside cylinder. The locomotive is numbered 822 and painted in SE&CR Grey livery. *Stephenson Locomotive Society*

Below: In 1931, No A822 was rebuilt with a third set of Walschaerts valve gear replacing the conjugating gear. At the same time, front footsteps were fitted. It was renumbered 1822 and smoke deflector plates were fitted. The embellishment on the smokebox door is unusual for an SR locomotive at this date. *Stephenson Locomotive Society*

Above: The prototype 'N1' 2-6-0, now in SR service as No A822 but still carrying the SE&CR plate on the side of the cab. *Ian Allan Library*

Right: No A890, the only three-cylinder 'K1' class 2-6-4T, *River Frome* was completed at Ashford in December 1925. Like the 'N1' No 822 (above), conjugated valve gear is fitted. Access to the motion is by means of the large steps. The perilous bar-mounted steps are still provided for access to the water filler. *Author's collection*

Below: When No A890 was rebuilt as the first 'U1' class in June 1928, the conjugated valve gear, wide cab and platform were retained. The curious shape of the cab-front 'spectacles' is clearly visible. No A890 now has a flat-topped dome to the firebox. *Ian Allan Library*

Above: In December 1931, No A890 was rebuilt with a third set of Walschaerts valve gear. At the same time, the platform was reduced in width, but the step down behind the cylinders was retained. A standard narrow cab was provided and front footsteps replaced those alongside the motion. The locomotive was renumbered 1890 and smoke deflectors were probably added at the same time. *Author's collection*

- For a given power requirement, the cylinders can be smaller than those on a two-cylinder locomotive, reducing the width of the locomotive.
- With six impulses per rotation of the wheels, the tractive force applied by the locomotive is more even than for a two-cylinder locomotive, with four impulses per rotation of the wheels.
- The rotating masses of a three-cylinder mechanism are largely self-balancing, avoiding the balance weights which are needed with two cylinders set at 90° to each other and thus reducing the hammer-blow effect on the track. In practice, some balancing was applied to three-cylinder locomotives at this time but, even so, the

rotating masses and balance weights were smaller than on a two-cylinder locomotive.

The first and third advantages also applied to four-cylinder locomotives in which the cranks were equally spaced at 90°. The main disadvantage was that a three-cylinder or four-cylinder locomotive was heavier and more expensive to build than an equivalent two-cylinder. There were also more components to maintain but the smoother running tended to reduce the wear and tear on the machinery. The potential width reduction offered a particular benefit on the Tonbridge to Hastings line of the SER. When the line was built, the contractor had skimped on the construction (inadequate brick lining) of a number of tunnels. By the

Below: 'N1' class No A880 in photographic grey was completed at Ashford in November 1930. The production batch of 'N1's were identical to the prototype, No 1822, with three sets of Walschaerts valve gear, but built without smoke deflectors. These were the only Maunsell Moguls to receive the flat-sided 4,000gal tender. *Ian Allan Library*

Above: 'N1' class No A878 as completed at Ashford, April 1930. *Ian Allan Library*

time the fault came to light, the only practical solution had been to insert additional rings of bricks inside the tunnel bore, restricting the loading gauge. While the SER and SE&CR used only small inside-cylinder locomotives this had not been a problem, but the new 'N' and 'K' class locomotives were too wide to use the line.

The Three-cylinder Prototypes

Two prototype three-cylinder locomotives were ordered from Ashford works in 1920, modified from one each of the 'N' and 'K' class locomotives which were already under construction. Class N1 2-6-0 No 822 was completed in March 1923 and Class K1 2-6-4T A890 *River Frome* in December 1925. Both had the Gresley/Holcroft derived motion but with a significant difference from Gresley's usual practice. On most of Gresley's three-cylinder locomotives, the conjugating levers were in front of the cylinders, driven by forward extensions of the valve spindles in the outside cylinders. Holcroft felt that this would cause problems with the valve setting as the valve rods expanded when hot. Gresley considered that this problem could be allowed for when setting up the valves but Holcroft provided an additional pair of rods, alongside the cylinders, connecting the outside valve gears to the combination levers. This added two more pin joints and two more rods to the system.

Apart from the additional cylinder, the prototype 'N1' class 2-6-0 No 822 differed from the 'N' class in having the boiler pitched 3in (76mm) higher and the platform alongside the boiler continued straight to the buffer beam, to cover the conjugating gear. Whilst all the other Maunsell Moguls ran with a boiler pressure of 200psi, No 822 ran at 190psi until 1925, probably to compensate for the cylinder volume being 6% higher than on the two-cylinder locomotives. The two-cylinder locomotives had sandboxes between the frames but No 822 had a sandbox mounted on the platform above each cylinder. Sandboxes in this position were carried by all the three-cylinder locomotives. All the three-cylinder locomotives had cab front 'spectacles' shaped to fit the firebox shoulders, without the additional round 'spectacles' of the 'N' and 'K' classes. The conjugated valve gear proved not to be satisfactory and was replaced by three sets of Walschaerts gear in 1931, the locomotive being renumbered from A822 to 1822 at the same time. The footsteps attached to the motion brackets were replaced by front-mounted footsteps.

Above: No 31898, a 'U1' class leaving Southampton Central on the Brighton–Bournemouth through train in September 1957. The BR standard carriages are all finished in carmine and cream livery. *Colour-Rail (BRS414)*

The three-cylinder 2-6-4T No A890 also differed from the 'K' class in having the boiler pitched 3in (76mm) higher and having the platform raised over the cylinders, to cover the conjugated gear. The cut-out in the tank, to give access to the motion, was much larger on the 'K' class and the single footstep on a round section bar was replaced by a large steel plate with three semicircular footholes, with a grab rail on the tank side. The front cab 'spectacles' were shaped to fit the firebox, as on No A822.

Following the Sevenoaks accident, No A890 *River Frome* was rebuilt as an unnamed 2-6-0 of Class U1, returning to traffic in June 1928, initially retaining conjugated valve gear and the wide platform and cab. The conjugated gear was replaced by an inside set of Walschaerts in December 1931 and the locomotive renumbered No 1890. Probably at the same time, the cab and platform were reduced in width, enabling it to run over the restricted Tonbridge to Hastings line. The front-mounted footsteps replaced the footstep alongside the motion.

Production 'N1' and 'U1' class 2-6-0s

Five more 'N1' class 2-6-0s were ordered from Ashford works in 1928 and delivered in 1930 with the numbers Nos A876 to A880. They were identical to No 1822, as modified with an inside set of Walschaerts valve gear.

As described above, the first of the 'U1' class 2-6-0s was No A890, rebuilt from the 'K1' class 2-6-4T in 1928. Ten further 'U1s' were ordered from Eastleigh works in 1928 and another 10 in 1929. These were all delivered during 1931 and were numbered A891-A900 and 1901-1910, the Southern's numbering system having changed halfway through the build. The new 'U1s' were basically identical to the prototype No 1890, as modified with an inside set of Walschaerts gear, but the platform alongside the boiler was straight, without the drop behind the cylinders which No 1890 retained throughout, and the cab and rear overhang were 5in (127mm) shorter than on No 1890.

The two prototype three-cylinder locomotives were coupled to 3,500gal (15,911-litre) tenders, but the production 'N1s' and 'U1s' all had the larger 4,000gal (18,184-litre) tender. Whilst the two cylinder 'U' class locomotives and the '14xx' series 'Ns' were provided with double slidebars, single slidebars were considered adequate for all the three-cylinder locomotives.

Above: The Southern Railway's official portrait of No A891, the first production 'U1', completed at Eastleigh in January 1931. This is a typical Eastleigh works photograph, taken alongside the Portsmouth line with the background hidden by a white board. No A891 differs from the rebuilt prototype No 1890. The platform is straight and the overhang is shorter, as is the cab. A 4,000gal tender with turned-in coal retaining plates is fitted. Initially, smoke deflectors were not fitted. *Ian Allan Library*

Below: The second 10 'U1s' of the production batch were completed after the SR had replaced the A-prefixed numbering by 1xxx numbers. No 1905 was completed at Eastleigh in August 1931. *Author's collection*

Right: The 'W' class 2-6-4T was effectively a small-wheeled version of the 'K1' class 2-6-4T No A890. The shape of the tanks is the same, as is the prominant footstep in front of the motion. No 1913 was completed at Eastleigh in January 1932. The driver was on the right-hand side and gravity sanding was fitted. No 1913 is painted in the goods livery of black with light green lining of the period. *Ian Allan Library*

Below right: 'W' class No 1917 was from the second batch and was completed at Ashford in April 1935. As the reversing rod is hidden, only the position of the vacuum ejector pipe shows that it is fitted for left-hand drive. Steam sanding is now fitted. *Ian Allan Library*

The 'W' class 2-6-4Ts

The final locomotives to be added to the Maunsell Mogul family were the three-cylinder goods tank engines of the 'W' class. These were built to allow freight trains in the electrified area around London to be speeded up, to keep out of the way of the frequent electric trains. They were a small-wheeled version of the 'K1' class 2-6-4T and it has been stated that they reused some components, such as tanks and bogies, removed from the 'K' and 'K1' locomotives when these were rebuilt. Side window cabs were fitted and, unusually for British practice, steam brakes were provided on the bogies. Five locomotives, Nos 1911-15, were delivered from Eastleigh works in 1932 and 10 more, Nos 1916-25, from Ashford in 1935-6. There were differences between the two batches, Nos 1911-15 had right-hand drive and gravity sanding, whilst 1916-25 had left-hand drive and steam sanding.

CHAPTER FIVE

Modifications

The main modifications to the Maunsell Moguls
were the rebuilding of 2-6-4Ts as 2-6-0s with tenders at the start
of their career, and the provision of new frames and
cylinders towars the end. Many other modifications and
experiments were tried in the years between.

This chapter describes the modifications carried out over the years on the Southern Railway locomotives of the Maunsell Mogul family. Modifications to the Irish and Metropolitan locomotives are described in the chapters which deal with these locomotives. The most important modification carried out to the Maunsell Moguls, the rebuilding of the 'K' and 'K1' class 2-6-4Ts to 'U' and 'U1' class 2-6-0s, has already been described. The second most important was the provision of new frames, or part frames, for many of the 'N' and 'U' class 2-6-0s between 1955 and 1961. The most noticeable modification was the fitting of smoke deflector plates to all the 2-6-0s during the 1930s. Over the years, many other modifications were carried out on the locomotives. These are covered approximately in the order in which they were applied.

Lamp irons
In common with the other constituent companies of the Southern Railway, the SE&CR used route codes to identify its trains but used only four lamp or disc positions whilst the LB&SCR and LSWR used six. The prototype 'N' class No 810 and 'K' class 2-6-4T No 790 were built with one lamp iron above the smokebox door and three on the buffer beam. Around 1920, two additional lamp irons were fitted, low down on either side of the smokebox, anticipating the introduction of six-disc route codes by the Southern Railway in April 1923. 'N' and 'N1' 2-6-0s Nos 811-825 were built with these additional brackets. This

arrangement was then used on all SR locomotives in the Maunsell Mogul family. The top lamp iron was moved down onto the smokebox door in the late 1930s. The three locomotives (Nos 1625, 1797 and 1831) fitted for oil burning in 1947 had electric lamps, surmounted by disc brackets, across the buffer beam and on the rear of the tender. The smokebox top electric lamp was in the original top bracket position. The smokebox side lamps were bracketed to the side of the smokebox front, just above the smoke deflector plates.

Mechanical lubricators
The two SE&CR prototypes, 'K' class No 790 and 'N' class No 810, were built with mechanical lubricators on the platform over the left side cylinder. These were removed around 1923 but similar lubricators appeared on No A847 (removed by 1939) and No A852 (until withdrawal), also Nos 31857 and 31870 in BR days. After smoke deflectors were fitted, the mechanical lubricators were positioned above the leading end of the left side valve rod guide. Metropolitan 2-6-4Ts were provided with similar lubricators. Three Moguls on the Mid-Hants Railway have been fitted with mechanical lubricators during preservation.

Slidebars
The two SE&CR prototypes 'K' No 790 and 'N' No 810 were built with a single slidebar to each cylinder, above

Above: 'N' class No 818 at Bricklayers Arms shed, August 1922, was completed at Ashford in March 1922. A stovepipe chimney is fitted for trials of different exhaust arrangements. No cylinder tailrods are fitted, an alteration made only to this locomotive. *Ian Allan Library*

Below: 'U1' class No 1892, in Maunsell Dark Green livery, at Waterloo in the mid 1930s. *Ian Allan Library*

the piston rod. Most of the SE&CR and Woolwich-built 'Ns' had single slidebars but Nos A843, A847 and s1825 are noted from photographs to have had double slidebars, although it is not known whether they were built with them or acquired them subsequently. 'K' class A790 was fitted with double slidebars around 1924 and the Southern-built 'Ks' and 'Us' were all built with double slidebars. The final batch of 'Ns' Nos 1400-1414 were built with double slidebars. The three-cylinder locomotives all had single slidebars.

Chimney

The SE&CR 'N' and 'K' class locomotives were built with a narrow chimney, based on recent Derby practice, with the outer casing flared into the base. The chimney on the 'K' class was taller than that of the 'N' and had no capuchon. The published weight diagrams show a height to the top of the chimney of 12ft 7in (3.84m) on the 'N' and 12ft 11⅜in (3.95m) on the 'K'. There were some steaming problems with the 'N' class and a blastpipe similar to that used on the GWR '43xx' class was trialled on four 'Ns' using stovepipe chimneys over the following periods (see table).

A wider chimney, with less flare into the base than the Derby pattern, was fitted to some on the SE&CR, the prototype 'N1' 2-6-0 No 822 and 'K1' 2-6-4T A890. No

Above: 'N' class A857 was built at Woolwich Arsenal then completed at Ashford in April 1925. A857 is at Exmouth Junction shed, *circa* 1930. After all the trials with a different chimney on the SE&CR, the Woolwich locomotives were delivered with the original narrow chimney, apparently with no ill effect on performance. The wider chimney was fitted when a replacement was required. A857 has two modifications: the cylinder by-pass valves have been removed and front footsteps have replaced the ones fixed to the motion bracket. The piston tailrods are retained.
Ian Allan Library

A790, a 'K' 2-6-4T, was so fitted around 1923. The Woolwich 'Ns' and the Southern-built 'Ks', 'N1s' and 'Us' reverted to the flared chimney, apparently without problems. The wider chimney was fitted to the '14xx' series 'Ns', the 'U1s' and the 'Ws' and was used as a replacement to the flared chimney on the other classes as a new chimney was required.

When the frame replacement exercise was carried out on the 'N' and 'U' classes in the 1950s, most of the re-framed locomotives received new blastpipes based on those used on the BR Standard Class 4 2-6-0. Some locomotives retained the Maunsell wide chimney, with a liner riveted inside it, but others, including some which retained their original frames, received the taller Class 4-type chimney. At least 13 of the 'U1' class were fitted with new blastpipes, with a sleeve in the Maunsell chimney. To the modeller, the blastpipe is invisible but the chimney is very distinctive. Locomotives fitted with Standard Class 4 chimneys are denoted in the tables at the end of the book by a letter (B) against the withdrawal date.

No	Stovepipe (fitted)	Stovepipe (removed)
812	January 1921	September 1923
817	January 1922	May 1923
818	August 1922	September 1922
819	May 1922	December 1924

Above: 'N' class No 1834 at Exmouth Junction, 9 June 1935. Smoke deflector plates are fitted, with a vertical grab rail at the bottom and a round hand hole towards the top of the front edge. Piston tailrods are retained. *Stephenson Locomotive Society*

Footsteps

Apart from conventional footsteps below the cab, the prototype 'N' and 'N1' class 2-6-0s were provided with a single footstep on the end of a length of round-section steel bar fixed to the motion bracket. This would have allowed the driver to step up to lubricate the motion but would not have provided access to the platform. The prototype 'K'

class 2-6-4T was provided with a similar step and another, to the rear of the driving axle, with two steps and two grab rails on the side tank, to give access to the tank fillers. These arrangements were perpetuated on the SE&CR- and Woolwich-built 'Ns' and also on the Southern-built 'K' class 2-6-4Ts. The solitary 'K1' class 2-6-4T, No A890,

Below: The 'N' class Nos 1407-1414 were built with smoke deflectors which had a horizontal grab rail at the bottom and a hand hole immediately above. The smoke deflectors on No 1408 have been modified, (probably soon after it was built) with a vertical grab rail and a second hand hole. Not all the 1407-1414 series had this modification. *Author's collection*

had the same arrangement as the 'K' class for filling the tanks but had a prominent set of steps, made up of a steel plate with three semicircular foot holes and a grab rail on the tank side, for access to the motion.

When the 2-6-4Ts were rebuilt as 2-6-0s, the steps giving access to the tank fillers were removed but the forward steps were initially unchanged. The 'A6xx' series 'Us' were built with conventional footsteps below the front drop of the running plate. These were also provided on the '14xx' series 'Ns' and replaced the steps on the motion on the earlier 'Ns' and 'Us' around 1931/2. When the prototype 'N1' and 'U1' had the conjugating gear removed, conventional footsteps were fitted, with three steps, at the front of the running plate. Similar steps were provided on the later 'N1', 'U1' and 'W' classes, whilst 'U1' No 1890 had the steps in front of the motion removed and front steps fitted. The 'W' class were built with both sets of steps.

Sandboxes
On the two-cylinder Moguls and 2-6-4Ts, the sandboxes were inside the frames, to the rear of the cylinders. On most of the 2-6-0s, these were filled directly by a man crouching on the platform. As access was impeded by the side tanks, the sandboxes on the 'K' class 2-6-4Ts were provided with curved filling pipes, emerging from between the tank front and the smokebox. When the 2-6-4Ts were rebuilt as 2-6-0s, the filling pipes were retained on the Eastleigh and Brighton rebuilds, Nos A790-A796, A801, A803, A804, A806-A809. These were removed on the Ashford rebuilds, Nos A797-A800, A802 and A805. The

Above: 'U' class No 1801, a 'Rebuilt River' in the mid-1930s. Smoke deflectors similar to those on the 'N' class but with an elongated hand hole towards the top of the front edge are fitted. *H. C. Casserley*

Brighton-built 'Us' Nos A610-A619 also had the curved filling pipes.

On all the three-cylinder 2-6-0s and 2-6-4Ts, the sandboxes were mounted on the platform to the rear of the cylinders.

Piston tailrods and cylinders
The two-cylinder Moguls and 2-6-4Ts were all built with piston tailrods except for No 818 and the '14xx' series of 'N' class. None of the three-cylinder locomotives had piston tailrods and those on the two-cylinder locomotives were removed in 1931/2, around the same time that front footsteps were fitted.

The two-cylinder locomotives, except for the 'A6xx' series 'Us' and '14xx' series 'Ns', had pressure relief valves, combined with cylinder by-pass valves, below the cylinders. The three-cylinder locomotives and the 'A6xx' and '14xx' series had pressure relief valves without by-pass valves, and the two-cylinder locomotives were subsequently modified in 1931/2.

Boilers
The boilers fitted to the Maunsell Mogul family were all interchangeable but there were internal differences, such as the size of the superheater, tube arrangement and steam

Above: No 1902, a three-cylinder 'U1' class 2-6-0, in the late 1930s. The smoke deflectors fitted to the 'U1' class had a vertical grab rail at the bottom of the front face with an elongated hand hole at the top of the grab rail. A further modification made in the 1930s is that the top lamp bracket has been moved down, onto the smokebox door.
Author's collection

supply to the regulator, which do not concern the modeller. One external difference was the dome casing, which was rounded on earlier boilers but flattened on later versions. Rounded domes were on the boilers carried initially by 'N' class Nos 810-824 and A825-A875, 'N1' class No 822 and A876-A880, and also 'K' class Nos 790 and A791-A809, as well as 'K1' class No A890. Flat-top domes were on the boilers initially fitted to 'N' class Nos. 1400 to 1414, 'U1' class Nos A891-A900 and Nos 1901-1910. 'U' class Nos A630-A639 and 'W' class Nos 1911-1925. As boilers were exchanged, both types of dome appeared on all classes.

Smoke deflector plates

As locomotive boilers became larger and the chimney shorter during the first quarter of the 20th century, problems began to occur with the exhaust smoke drifting alongside the boiler and obscuring the driver's line of sight. The provision of plates alongside the smokebox to direct a stream of clean air along the side of the boiler was first tried out in Germany in the early 1920s and adopted by the Southern Railway, initially on the 'King Arthur' class 4-6-0s, in 1928.

During the development of the 'Schools' class 4-4-0s, wind tunnel tests with models were carried out at the National Physical Laboratory to try out different forms of smoke deflector. A model of a Mogul was tested at the same time, leading to a modified form of deflector plate, with the leading edge further forward with a cutaway at the bottom to provide a toehold for anyone walking around the locomotive's platform. These modified plates were fitted to the 'Schools' and Moguls. The only Moguls to be built with smoke deflectors were Nos 1407-1414. The rest of the Moguls were fitted with deflector plates around 1934-6.

There were a number of variations to the smoke deflectors. Those fitted new to 'Ns' Nos 1407 and 1410-1414 had a horizontal grab rail above the front footstep and a rectangular hand hole above, in the front edge of the deflector. Similar plates were fitted to 'N' class Nos 1816 and 1850 and to 'U' No A629 when burning pulverized coal. The recess at the front bottom corner was not on A629. No 1410 had extensions to the top edge of the plates (see p66). No 1408 had a vertical grab rail and two hand holes in the front edge of the plate, but it is not known whether it was built like this or modified. In BR days, Nos. 31407 and 31409 were similar.

The 'standard' arrangement, fitted to the rest of the 'Ns' and the '16xx' series 'U' class had a vertical grab rail and a single round hand hole at the top of the straight part of the front edge of the plate. The plates on Nos 1790-1809 series 'U's were similar but with rectangular hand holes. On most of the Nos 1790-1809 series, the plates were set the same distance apart as on the narrow platform

locomotives, giving a greater width of platform outside the deflectors. Photographs of Nos 1795, 1797, 1799, 1801, 1805 and 1806 show the plates set wider apart, with the same width of platform outside the deflectors as on the narrow platform 2-6-0s. Those fitted with new cylinders in the 1950s all had the deflectors set in, behind the snifting valve casing. The plates on the 'N1' and 'U1' classes were as those on Nos 1790-1809 series 'U' class but with straight lower edges.

Snifting valves

All locomotives with Maunsell's design of superheater, including all the Mogul family, had two snifting valves on either side of the smokebox behind the chimney. Bulleid carried out tests which indicated that these valves were not worthwhile and had them removed around 1948/50.

The new cylinders, with outside live steampipes, fitted to a number of 'N' and 'U' class 2-6-0s during the 1950s had a snifting valve on the top of each cylinder. On the 'Ns' and '316xx' series 'Us', this was behind a projecting casing on the side of the platform but on the Nos 31790 to 31809 series 'Us', the casing was on top of the platform.

New frames and cylinders

The Maunsell Moguls were built down to a strict weight limit to suit the SE&CR tracks of the early 20th century. The frames were not as robust as might be desired and frequent repairs were necessary on the two-cylinder

Above: 'N' class No 1402 at Ashford in 1948. This locomotive was built in 1932 without smoke deflectors but now has the type with a vertical grab rail and a round hand hold. The top lamp bracket has been lowered. The snifting valves have been removed, a modification applied to all locomotives with Maunsell superheaters between 1946 and 1950. The livery is unlined Black with Green shaded 'Sunshine'-style lettering. *J. H. Aston*

Above right: No 31848 at Tonbridge, 3 November 1956, was the first of the 28 'N' and 22 'U' class 2-6-0s which was fitted with new full, or front, frames between October 1955 and May 1961. The wide Maunsell chimney, with an internal sleeve to suit the BR blastpipe, is retained. Note the rivets fixing the sleeve to the chimney. No 31848 ran until February 1957 without smoke deflectors. The lack of smoke deflectors enables the cladding over the live steampipe to be seen, as well as the convex curve to the top edge of the main frame above the front drop. A grab rail has been fixed to the platform above the front footstep. *P. T. Abbott*

locomotives. There was less of a problem with the more even torque of the three-cylinder locomotives. In the 1950s, it was perceived that the Moguls still had some years to run and, in 1954, Ashford works was authorised to provide new frames for the worst examples of 'N' and 'U' class locomotives. Depending on the condition of the frames, new full length frames or front end frames were provided. In either case, new cylinders with outside live steampipes and the blastpipe of the BR Standard Class 4

were used. Some locomotives retained the Maunsell chimney but others received the taller Standard Class 4 chimney. The first 'N' to receive new frames, No 31848 in October 1955, was not fitted with smoke deflectors but these were fitted in February 1957. Apart from the outside steampipe, the new frames were recognisable by having a

'N' Full Frame	Date	'N' Front Frame	Date	'U' Full Frame	Date	'U' Front Frame	Date
No 31406 (B)	1/1960	No 31400 (B)	1/1958	No 31615 (B)	6/1960	No 31613 (B)	3/1958
No 31413 (B)	5/1960	No 31405	3/1957	No 31621	2/1955	No 31614	2/1957
No 31829	10/1960	No 31408 (B)	4/1957	No 31625 (B)	1/1959	No 31617 (B)	2/1961
No 31833 (B)	6/1959	No 31830	11/1955	No 31628	1/1957	No 31622 (B)	11/1960
No 31835 (B)	5/1957	No 31831 (B)	8/1960	No 31631	10/1960	No 31623	3/1956
No 31837 (B)	2/1961	No 31838 (B)	6/1957	No 31634	4/1955	No 31624	5/1956
No 31845 (B)	3/1960	No 31840	2/1957	No 31637 (B)	10/1959	No 31633 (B)	9/1960
No 31848	10/1955	No 31842 (B)	12/1957	No 31791 (B)	4/1960	No 31635 (B)	1/1959
No 31855	12/1955	No 31843 (B)	8/1958	No 31796 (B)	1/1961	No 31792 (B)	10/1958
No 31858 (B)	6/1961	No 31846 (B)	5/1959	No 31809 (B)	9/1960	No 31795 (B)	2/1958
No 31871 (B)	3/1961	No 31853 (B)	7/1960			No 31802 (B)	1/1958
		No 31854 (B)	8/1857			No 31806 (B)	11/1957
		No 31862 (B)	4/1960				
		No 31864 (B)	1/1959				
		No 31868 (B)	12/1960				
		No 31869 (B)	2/1958				
		No 31874 (B)	5/1957				

Above: Photographed at Eastleigh, 17 August 1962 'U' class No 31791 was fitted with full new frames in April 1960. The taller BR Standard Class 4-type chimney is fitted. The live steampipe is hidden by the smoke deflectors but the convex curve to the frame is visible. No 31791 is also fitted with AWS and has overhead warning flashes on its smoke deflectors and firebox. The AWS battery and reservoir are mounted at the side of the firebox and the receiver is on the leading truck. Note the protective 'bash' plate below the buffer beam. *John Scrace*

convex curve to the top of the visible section of frame above the front drop of the running plate, and were 4½in (114mm) longer than the original frames. The table on page 41 shows the dates at which locomotives received frame conversions. Those marked (B) also received a Standard Class 4 chimney, but No 31846 reverted to a Maunsell chimney in September 1960. Nos 31614 and 31624 had a Maunsell chimney when modified but later received Standard Class 4 chimney in December and June 1961 respectively.

Automatic Warning System

British Railways Automatic Warning System (AWS) was installed on some Southern Region lines from the late 1950s. At each distant signal, a permanent magnet and an electromagnet were placed between the rails. If the signal was at danger, a receiver on the locomotive sensed the

Below: No 31916 'W' class at Eastleigh shed. No 31916 was fitted with AWS equipment in September 1962. The battery box and reservoir are mounted below the cab on the fireman's side (No 31916 has left-hand drive whilst the unidentified 'W' class locomotive behind has right-hand drive). There are no conduits for electrical cabling visible, suggesting that the receiver was probably mounted on the trailing bogie. *Author's collection*

Above: No A819 was completed in May 1922 with a Worthington-Simpson feedwater heater and pump mounted on the left-hand platform. The equipment was used until November 1928. *Ian Allan Library*

permanent magnet and, unless the driver cancelled the warning straight away, applied the vacuum brake. The inrush of air to the brake sounded a horn in the cab. If the signal was clear, the electromagnet was energised and cancelled the warning, sounding a bell in the cab. On the Moguls, the AWS receiver was mounted on the leading truck, with a 'bash' plate fixed to the buffer beam to protect the receiver from the coupling. A battery box and air reservoir were mounted on the running plate, beside the firebox, on the driver's side. On the two 'W' class 2-6-4Ts fitted with AWS (Nos 31916 and 31922), the battery box and reservoir were mounted under the cab on

the fireman's side and it is thought that the receiver was probably mounted on the trailing bogie.

Short-term experiments

A number of experiments were carried out on Maunsell Moguls. Space constraints limit what can be written here about these but can be summarised as:

A Worthington-Simpson feedwater heater and pump were fitted to 'N' class No A819 between May 1922 and November 1928. During these trials, No A819 was fitted with a wide chimney as fitted to 'N1' class No 822. There

Below: Between completion in December 1929 and October 1932, 'U' class No A629 was fitted with an automatic stoker to burn pulverised coal. Smoke deflectors were fitted in October 1931, probably the first Maunsell Mogul to be so fitted. No A629 is under the fuel hopper at Eastbourne shed after coaling. *Ian Allan Library*

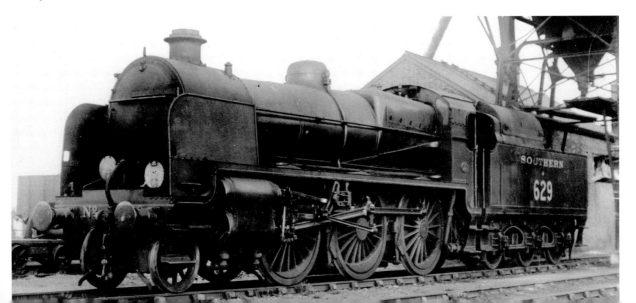

Above: Between August 1931 and May 1935, A816 was used for testing a system in which the exhaust steam was cooled, then compressed and fed back to the boiler. The 'side tanks' contain the cooler and the compressor, driven by a totally enclosed three-cylinder steam engine, mounted alongside the firebox. The equipment was fitted on both sides of the locomotive. *Ian Allan Library*

was a saving of about 2½lbs (1.13kg) of coal per train mile but Maunsell considered that this did not justify the cost and complication of the equipment, including three failures in traffic.

Pulverised fuel trials, using German-designed equipment, were carried out on 'U' class No A629 between December 1929 and October 1932. An enclosed bunker and cab were fitted to the tender with steam-driven feed screws to deliver the coal to the firebox where it was blown in by an air blast provided by a steam turbine-driven

fan. There were no firebars and the lower part of the firebox was lined with firebrick. After initial trials from Ashford, the locomotive was based at Eastbourne, where an enclosed coal bunker was provided. During 20 months of trials, No A629 ran only 3,497 miles (2,628km).

Steam heat conservation trials were carried out on 'N' class No A816 between August 1931 and May 1935. Using a system designed by Scottish marine engineer H. Anderson, all the exhaust steam was passed into a cooler and was then compressed before being returned to the boiler. As there was no conventional steam exhaust, draught for the fire was provided by a fan driven by a high speed steam engine on the smokebox door. For a period during 1933, a square chimney was fitted. The system

Below: At this stage, a rectangular chimney is fitted and the fan engine has been removed. *H. C. Casserley*

Above: No 1797 'U' class running as an oil burner, with electric lighting, at Fratton (Portsmouth), 11 September 1948. The oil tank could be placed directly into the coal space of the later 3,500gal tender. The electric lights on the smokebox are mounted higher than the standard lamp irons. Those across the buffer beam have the lamp irons above. A tail oil lamp has been placed above the left-hand electric light, probably for a tender-first light engine movement. *H. C. Casserley / R. J. Hardy collection*

showed some promise but the promoters ran out of money before the trials were completed.

Marshall valve gear, designed by J. T. Marshall of Harrogate, was fitted to 'N' class No 1850 between October 1933 and March 1934. Steam admission to the cylinders was by conventional piston valves but exhaust was controlled by separate slide valves below the cylinders. The locomotive was rebuilt and the trials conducted from Eastleigh. Some saving was shown at low speeds compared with the standard arrangement but a knock developed at speeds over about 50mph (80kph). The valve gear finally disintegrated when running on a passenger train near Woking on 22 March 1934.

Oil burning

Oil burning by steam locomotives was proposed by the government during 1947, to overcome coal shortages. The Southern converted a number of locomotives including two 'U' and one 'N' class 2-6-0s. A 1,600gal (7,272-litre) oil tank, with the top edges chamfered to fit the loading gauge, was placed in the coal space of the 3,500gal (15,911-litre) tender. 'U' class Nos 1625 and 1797 ran as oil burners from October 1947 to September 1948, and 'N' class No 1831 from September 1947 to September 1948. The locomotives were fitted with electric lighting in January 1948 but this was removed, some time after reverting to coal burning. The oil burning scheme failed due to the lack of foreign currency to buy the oil.

Below: 'N' class No 1850, fitted with Marshall valve gear, fitted in February 1934. Steam admission is by piston valves but exhaust is controlled by slide valves under the cylinders. Two sets of reversing gear are fitted, requiring the cab to be widened on the driver's side and the lower part extended forward. Smoke deflectors of the type fitted to Nos 1407-14 are fitted. These are, unusually, painted black. *Ian Allan Library*

CHAPTER SIX

Tenders

Two types of tender, with variants on each type,
were coupled to the Maunsell Moguls. Some exchange
of tenders occurred but many Moguls were coupled
to the same tender throughout service.

The prototype 'N' class 2-6-0 No 810 was coupled to the first of a new design of tender built at Ashford works. The chassis, with semicircular slots between the axleboxes, was similar to the tenders produced at Ashford during the 1900s for Wainwright's 4-4-0s and 0-6-0s. The tender body, with flat sides incorporating the coal retaining plates and with toolboxes set across the front of the tender, followed recent Midland Railway practice. The base of the tank was set 4ft 5in (1.35m) above rail level and had a capacity for 3,500gal (15,911 litres) of water and 5 tons (5,080kg) of coal. Footsteps, with curved inner edges to the backing plates, were fixed at all four corners of the tender with the upper part of the backing plate angled, to merge with the running plate valance. The tenders coupled to Nos 810-815 initially had only a single vacuum cylinder but a second was added later and the tenders of Nos 816-824 and A825 were built with two. The Woolwich tenders were built with a single vacuum cylinder but a second one was added before the locomotives went into service.

On the prototype tender coupled to No 810 and on the Woolwich-built tenders, the ends of the buffer beams were square but on the tenders coupled to Nos 811-824 and A825, they were angled, to follow the shape of the footstep backing plate. Buffers were the same as those on the front of the locomotives, with stepped parallel casings but some of the Woolwich-built tenders had tapered buffer housings, possibly provided from stock held at Ashford. A small horizontal grab rail was fitted above the front footsteps. A

set of three lockers or toolboxes was set across the front of the tender with the curved-topped front bulkhead of the coal bunker behind. A curved rail was set across the centre of the coal bunker, carrying a U-shaped bracket in the centre to hold fire irons, the handles of which were hooked over stanchions towards the centre of the front bulkhead. The fire iron stanchions and brackets were later moved closer to the sides of the tender.

Later 3,500gal (15,911-litre) tenders were built by Armstrong Whitworth and Ashford for rebuilding the 'K' and 'K1' class 2-6-4Ts into 'U' class Nos A610-A629 and A790-A809, and also 'U1' class No A890. These had angled ends to the buffer beams and stepped parallel buffer casings. At the front of the tender, there were only two toolboxes, set closer to the sides of the tender than those on the SE&CR or Woolwich tenders. There was a space between them, and the front bulkhead of the coal bunker was straight, at the level of the front of the tender sides. The fire iron stanchions were fixed to the back of the toolboxes and the retaining brackets were fixed inside the coal plates. There was a vertical water gauge outside the left front of the tender body. The front grab rail was vertical. During the rebuilding exercise, some of the Ashford rebuilds Nos A797-A802, A805 and A890 received tenders from 'N' class Moguls, whilst 'N' class Nos A814, A829, A837 and A874 received the later type tender. During the 1960s, tenders from 'L1' class 4-4-0s were coupled to some Moguls. These were similar to the

Above: A Woolwich-built 3,500gal tender of 'N' class locomotive No A874. A row of three lockers was fitted across the front of the tender. The fire irons are located by two stanchions towards the centre of the front bulkhead. A horizontal grab rail is mounted above the front footsteps. *Ian Allan Library*

Below: Woolwich 3,500gal tender of 'N' class No 1854. This was one of two 'Ns' to receive Bulleid's Apple Green livery in 1946. The tender has BRITISH RAILWAYS in 'Sunshine' livery and the number 31854 on the rear. There are now two fire iron stanchions at either end of the front bulkhead. The brackets over the coal space have also been moved to the ends of the transverse rail. *Author's collection*

Above: 'U' class 2-6-0 No A617 is coupled to one of the later 3,500gal tenders. A water gauge is fitted at the front of the tender on the fireman's side. The grab rail above the footstep is now vertical. There are now only two toolboxes/lockers at the front of the tender and the front bulkhead of the coal space is the same height as the low part of the tender side. The fire iron brackets are now fixed directly to the coal plates. *Ian Allan Library*

Below: Photographic grey image of the 4,000gal tender of 'N' class 2-6-0 No 1410. Although Nos 1407-1414 were built with left-hand drive, the tenders were built for right-hand drive, with the tender handbrake on the driver's side. The arrangement of the toolboxes and fire iron supports is similar to that on the later 3,500gal tenders. Tenders with the handbrake on the right (fireman's) side were supplied in 1937/8. *Ian Allan Library*

Above: The 4,000gal tender of 'U1' class No A898 at Portsmouth Harbour, 6 June 1931. Note the curved rear corners of the tender and the numberplate on the rear. The plate was replaced by transfer numerals when the A-suffix was removed, later in 1931. *H. C. Casserley*

SE&CR tenders coupled to Nos 811-824 and A825 but had the water gauge and vertical grab rail of later tenders.

4,000 gallon tender

A new design of 4,000gal (18,184 litre) six-wheeled tender was introduced during 1928. The first of these were built to run with 'Lord Nelson' class 4-6-0s, Nos E851-E860 but only two of them ran, briefly, with these locomotives. The new tender was a six-wheeled version of the flat-sided type built at Eastleigh in 1927 for the prototype 'Lord Nelson' class 4-6-0 No E850. It was wider than the Ashford 3,500gal (15,911-litre) tender with the base of the tank set 4ft 0in (1.23m) above rail level, following Eastleigh practice. The rear corners of the tank were curved whereas on the 3,500gal (15,911-litre) type, the sides and rear met at a right angle. The arrangement of the toolboxes and fire iron brackets was as on the later 3,500gal (15,911-litre) type. The depth of the side frames was reduced between the axleboxes, with no slots. Tenders of this type were coupled to 'U' class 2-6-0s Nos A630-A639, 'N1' class Nos A876-A880, 'U1' class Nos

A891-A900 and Nos 1901-1910, and also 'N' class Nos 1400-1414. In all cases where these tenders were coupled to a Maunsell Mogul, the running plate was joggled upwards at the front to match the rear drop of the locomotive running plate.

There were two variants of this tender, with a third variant added later. The tenders attached to the 'U', 'U1' and 'N' classes had the coal plates turned inwards whilst those coupled to 'N1s' Nos A876-A880 had straight sides. As the 'N1s' were able to run on the Tonbridge to Hastings line, the turned-in coal plates cannot have been a requirement of the Hastings line loading gauge. However, the turned-in plates would have brought the width at the top of the coal plates closer to that of the narrow cabs of the Moguls.

Tender exchanges

The following tender exchanges refer only to those which resulted in the type of tender attached to a locomotive being changed.

'U1' class No 1890 was involved in a shed collision in July 1932 which damaged the 3,500gal tender. It ran from July 1932 to October 1935 with the new 4,000gal (18,184-litre) tender (No 3066) which had been built for No 1401. Nos 1400/1401 left works with tender Nos 3065/3067.

'N' class 2-6-0s Nos 1407-1414 were built with left-hand drive but were coupled to 4,000gal (18,184-litre) tenders built for right-hand-drive locomotives. In 1937/8, new 4,000gal (18,184-litre) tenders to suit left-hand drive were built at Eastleigh.

'U' class locomotives No 1610 to 1629 received 4,000gal tenders with turned-in coal plates in 1938-9. Those coupled to Nos 1610-1617 came from 'N' class Nos 1407-1414, whilst those coupled to Nos 1618-1629 were built new at Eastleigh. The 3,500gal (15,911-litre) tenders from Nos 1610-1629 were coupled to new 'Q' class 0-6-0

Above: A 4,000gal tender on 'U' class No 31610 at Axminster, 14 May 1959. *A. E. West / South Western Circle*

locomotives. At this stage, all the Nos 1610-1639 series 'Us' had 4,000gal (18,184-litre) tenders and all the Nos 1790-1809 series had 3,500gal (15,911-litre) tenders. This was a curious arrangement as it coupled the wide tenders to the narrow cab locomotives and vice versa. In later years, there were numerous exchanges, the following being noted by Don Bradley:

The following additional tender exchanges are noted from photographs:

'U' 31808 with a 4,000gal in 3/1960
'N' 31870 with a 4,000gal in 8/1963
'N' 31410 with a 3,500gal in 10/1964. There were probably others.

A further 4,000gal (18,184 litre) tender is the one coupled to No 31806 on the Mid-Hants Railway. This has the appearance of the flat-sided tenders coupled to the 'N1' class 2-6-0s but is actually a tender from an 'S15' class 4-6-0, which has been modified at the front end to suit the right-hand drive locomotive.

Above : A 4,000gal flat-sided tender coupled to 'N1' class No A878. *Author's collection*

'1790' series with 4,000gal (18,184-litre) tender

No	From	To
31791	12/1962	Withdrawal
31798	1/1948	10/1957
31799	8/1957	Withdrawal
31800	5/1958	Withdrawal
31802	2/1944	5/1944
31803	10/1947	Withdrawal

'1790' series with 4,000gal (18,184-litre) tender

No	From	To
31804	5/1944	Withdrawal
31805	10/1947	Withdrawal
31806	3/1953	1/1957
31809	5/1945	Withdrawal

'1610' series with 3,500gal (15,911-litre) tender

No	From	To
31610	3/1953	6/1957
31613	9/1947	8/1962
31616	10/1957	Withdrawal
31618	2/1944	Withdrawal
31619	5/1946	Withdrawal
31625	12/1947	Withdrawal
31629	10/1947	Withdrawal
31638	10/1947	Withdrawal

CHAPTER SEVEN

Numbers, Names, Liveries

The successive owners of Maunsell Moguls,
the SE&CR, SR and British Railways, each applied
standard liveries but retained the running numbers
throughout, although with added characters.

This chapter deals only with the Southern Railway locomotives. Numeration and liveries of the Metropolitan and Irish-based railways are covered in the chapters dealing with those locomotives.

Numbers
Each locomotive in the SR Maunsell Mogul family went into service with a running number which was never altered, although successive owners added letters or numerals in front of the basic three-digit number.

The locomotives built by the SE&CR all carried a three-digit number. When the Southern Railway took over, it did not renumber the locomotives of its three constituent companies but added a letter prefix, A (Ashford) for ex-SE&CR locomotives, B (Brighton) for ex-LBSCR locomotives and E (Eastleigh) for ex-LSWR locomotives. New locomotives were given A, B or E prefixes depending on which workshop was to provide their heavy maintenance. All the Maunsell Mogul family were maintained at Ashford, so had A-prefix numbers. In mid-1931, the letter prefixes were abandoned. Most E-prefix numbers reverted to their three-digit number. Most A-prefix numbers had 1000 added, and B-prefix numbers had 2000 added. Ex-LSWR 'Duplicate' numbers in the E0xxx series had 3000 added, and the 'Z' class 0-8-0Ts, although built at Brighton, had A-prefix numbers but now reverted to their basic three-digit numbers.

When the railways were nationalised in 1948,

a few locomotives were given s-prefixes to the Southern number. British Railways then added 30000 to the numbers on Southern locomotives, although the remaining locomotives with 3xxx numbers were renumbered into the 30xxx series. Bulleid's locomotives had carried numbers as idiosyncratic as the locomotives themselves and were renumbered conventionally by British Railways into the 33xxx to 36xxx series.

For example, 'N' class 2-6-0 No 813 was new in September 1920 as SE&CR No 813. It became Southern No A813 in January 1926, Southern No 1813 after mid-1931 (exact date not known), British Railways No s1813 in February 1948 and No 31813 in June 1950.

Names
The Southern Railway had a policy of naming its express locomotives. As far as the Maunsell Mogul family is concerned, this policy applied only to the 'K' and 'K1' class 2-6-4Ts, which were named after rivers which flowed through Southern territory. Many river names occur in different parts of the country, such as Avon, which is basically the pre-Anglo Saxon word for a river (Afon or Afan) with the spelling and pronunciation anglicised. The list on page 55, showing the approximate route of the rivers commemorated, has been derived from an atlas of southern England, choosing those rivers which seem most likely where the same name occurs more than once. Some of the rivers are very obscure and the map does not clarify

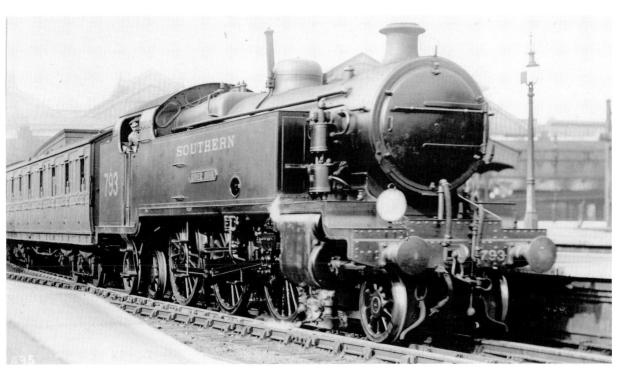

Above: 'K' class 2-6-4T No A793 *River Ouse* at Victoria on a Brighton train *circa* 1926. No A793 will cross its namesake river, by means of the magnificent Ouse Viaduct, shortly before Haywards Heath. The A-prefix is above the number on the tender. The buffer beam only carries the number 793 in small sans serif letters. *Author's collection*

Below: 'U1' class No A899 on a Bournemouth train in the Clapham Cutting *circa* 1931. No A899 is finished in Maunsell Green livery with black edging and white lining. Buffer beam numerals are now in large yellow serif-style characters, with the A suffix to the left of the coupling. *E. R. Wethersett*

which of the streams which form a river is to be regarded as the river itself. No A809 should surely be a Great Western locomotive, unless there is another Dart which I have not spotted. After the Sevenoaks accident, the newspapers quickly dubbed the 'K' class the 'Rolling Rivers'. It was therefore hardly surprising that the names were not perpetuated on 'U' class locomotives.

At the time the Maunsell Moguls were introduced, the previous ornate lined green livery of SE&CR locomotives had given way to unlined slate grey, relieved only by the running number in large white sanserif numerals on the tender or tank side and 'No' and the running number, in serif lettering, on either side of the coupling on the buffer beam. Ownership was displayed by a small cast plate

Above: No 1901 a 'U1' class locomotive at Waterloo in the 1930s. This was the first of the 'U1' class to be built, in June 1931, with a 19xx number. The buffer beam number is to the left of the coupling. *Ian Allan Library*

Below: 'U' class No 1795 at Yeovil shed, 29 August 1940. Although it is not possible to see whether the livery is green or black, the 1940 date suggests that it is in the unlined Maunsell Green with Bulleid-style 'Sunshine' lettering. *H. C. Casserley*

Below right: 'N' class No 1827 with a trainload of wagon kits, built at Ashford for Iran, 23 October 1941. The locomotive is in unlined black, with Bulleid-style lettering. The number is now on the cab side. A blackout screen is folded on the front of the tender. *Ian Allan Library*

No	Name	County	Towns passed through or near
A790	*River Avon*	Wilts/Hants	Amesbury, Salisbury, Ringwood, Christchurch
A791	*River Adur*	Sussex	Burgess Hill, Steyning, Shoreham
A792	*River Arun*	Sussex	Billingshurst, Pulborough, Arundel, Littlehampton
A793	*River Ouse*	Sussex	Haywards Heath, Lewes, Newhaven
A794	*River Rother*	Sussex/Kent	Mayfield, Robertsbridge, Rye
A795	*River Medway*	Kent	Tonbridge, Maidstone, Chatham, Rochester
A796	*River Stour*	Kent	Ashford, Canterbury, Sandwich
A797	*River Mole*	Surrey	Salfords, Dorking, Leatherhead, Molesey
A798	*River Wey*	Surrey	Farnham, Guildford, Weybridge
A799	*River Test*	Hants	Overton, Whitchurch, Romsey, Southampton
A800	*River Cray*	Kent	The Crays, Crayford
A801	*River Darenth*	Kent	Sevenoaks, Dartford
A802	*River Cuckmere*	Sussex	Hailsham, Alfriston, Cuckmere Haven
A803	*River Itchen*	Hants	Alresford, Winchester, Southampton
A804	*River Tamar*	Devon/Cornwall	Northeast of Bude, Launceston, Gunnislake, Saltash
A805	*River Camel*	Cornwall	Camelford, Bodmin, Wadebridge, Padstow
A806	*River Torridge*	Devon	Holsworthy, Torrington, Bideford
A807	*River Axe*	Devon	Chard, Axminster, Seaton
A808	*River Char*	Dorset	East of Axminster, Charmouth
A809	*River Dart*	Devon	Ashburton, Buckfastleigh, Totnes, Dartmouth
A890	*River Frome*	Dorset	Maiden Newton, Dorchester, Wareham

lettered SE&CR on the side of the cab or bunker. This livery was carried by 'K' class 2-6-4T 790 and 'N' and 'N1' class 2-6-0s Nos 810-824.

Southern Railway liveries to 1939

Initial Southern Railway liveries were based on those of the London & South Western Railway. Passenger locomotives were painted Olive Green (sometimes referred to as Sage Green) with black edging and white lining to the panels. Goods locomotives were black, replacing the LSWR Dark Green, with a light green line where the passenger locomotives had a white line. In February 1925, Maunsell adopted a darker shade of green for the passenger engines.

Reports in *Locomotive Magazine* suggest that some of the Woolwich locomotives were painted at first in the Southern's goods livery. John Harvey has drawn my attention to a report by a Brighton-based observer who visited Exeter in August 1924. He reports that, of some 10 'government 2-6-0s' in the Exeter area, No A832 was then in an unlined grey livery, with SOUTHERN lettering and the number on the tender in yellow, including painted cab

Above: 'U' class No 1613 and 'N' class No 1825 at Ashford in 1939, with ex-SE&CR 'J' class 0-6-2T No 1598 and 'H' class 0-4-4T No 1305. *Colour-Rail (SR61)*

side and tender plates. Apart from these short-lived oddities, all the Moguls, and the 'Rivers', carried the Maunsell Dark Green from new, whilst the 'W's always carried the goods black livery, lined on Nos 1911-1915 when new but unlined on the others.

Boiler, cab, splashers, platform valance and tender sides were green, with a fine white line between the green and the black edging, the green on the cab side extending up to the rainstrip at the level where the cab roof was extended back over the tender fallplate. Boiler bands were black with a fine white line either side, but with only one white line at the rear of the smokebox. There was black edging with a single white line on the front and rear vertical edges of the green cylinder cladding, later changed to a rectangular green panel. Wheels were green, with black tyres and axle ends. When smoke deflectors were

first fitted, Ashford painted them green on the Moguls until early 1938, after which they were black.

Lettering comprised the word SOUTHERN, 9ft 9in (2.97m) long in elongated 6½in (16.5cm) serif letters, on the tender or on the side tank. On the Moguls, the 'Ws' and No A790 before it was named, the locomotive number was applied below it in 18in (46cm) block figures, with the 3in (76mm) A prefix in between. On the named 'River' tanks, the number was on the side of the bunker and the nameplate was mounted below the SOUTHERN lettering. The lettering and numbers were in a primrose colour. The number appeared on the buffer beams, to the right of the coupling, in 6in (15.24cm) yellow serif numerals, with '*No.*' to the left of the coupling.

Below: 'U1' class No 1904 in Bulleid black livery, passing Bickley on a Ramsgate train in 1946. An ex SE&CR 'Trio' set has been strengthened by three 10 compartment thirds. *Ian Allan Library*

Above: 'W' class 2-6-4T No 1924 in Bulleid Black livery at Brighton, May 1948. *R. K. Blencowe*

Some ex-SE&CR locomotives continued to carry the SE&CR cast plates on the cabside but these was replaced by oval brass numberplates, 13⅝in x 7⅝in (34.6cm x 19.4cm) with the lettering SOUTHERN RAILWAY in an arc around the top of the plate, with the number below and the prefix between. A third plate was attached to the rear of the tender body. Tank engines had only a single plate, on the rear of the bunker.

When the prefixes were abandoned, new cab side plates were cast with SOUTHERN in an arc at the top of the plate, RAILWAY at the bottom, and the number between. The numberplates on the rear of the tenders or bunkers were replaced by transfer numerals. The backing colour of the number and nameplates was initially either green or black but by about 1926, red began to be used for

nameplates, No A890 *River Frome* being so treated. Red backed numberplates began to appear in mid-1928.

Southern Railway liveries from 1939 to 1948

When Oliver Bulleid succeeded Maunsell as the Southern's Chief Mechanical Engineer, he tried out a variety of brighter liveries on some of the express passenger locomotives but none of these were applied to the Moguls at this time. At the outbreak of World War 2, Moguls were repainted in unlined Dark Green, initially continuing the Maunsell-style lettering but later with Bulleid-style lettering. The following were noted by Don Bradley:

Below: 'N' class No 1817 and No 1854 were repainted in Bulleid's Malachite Green livery in September 1946 for working Victoria to Brighton trains via Uckfield. No 1854 is at Brighton on 28 April 1947. *F. M. Gates*

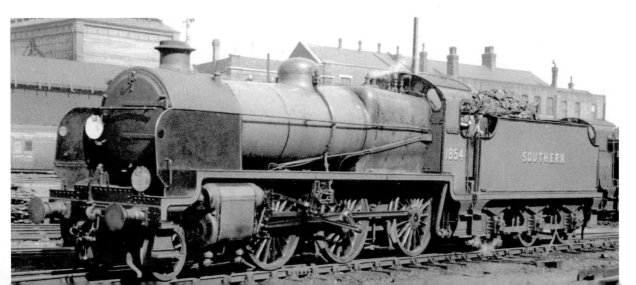

Above: 'U1' class No 31900 leaving Eastbourne on the 11.30 to Birmingham New Street, 10 June 1950. The unlined black locomotive retains the snifting valves. SOUTHERN is painted on the tender but the locomotive now has a British Railways number on a smokebox door plate and also on the cab side, in Bulleid-style numerals. The visible part of the train is made up of 1925 Thanet stock. *S. C. Nash*

Unlined Dark Green with Maunsell-style lettering (Sept 1939):
'U' class Nos 1624, 1625, 1635, 1806, 1807 and 1809
'N' class Nos 1407, 1413, 1414, 1850, 1856, 1863, 1877, 1891, 1894 and 1896
'U1' class No 1907

Unlined Dark Green with Bulleid-style lettering (Jan 1940):
'U' class Nos 1610, 1612, 1613, 1615, 1617-1620, 1623, 1625, 1627-1629, 1631, 1637, 1638, 1791, 1792, 1794, 1795, 1799, 1801, 1803 and 1805
'N' class Nos 1400, 1403, 1408, 1409, 1810, 1813, 1818,

1820, 1821, 1823, 1825, 1826, 1828, 1841, 1847, 1848, 1854, 1858, 1867, 1868, 1870, 1874 and 1875
'N1' class Nos 1876, 1878 and 1879
'U1' class Nos 1890, 1892, 1895, 1897, 1898, 1901, 1902, 1904 and 1909.

From March 1941 all the Moguls were painted unlined black with Bulleid-style lettering. This livery was retained until 1948 with two exceptions. In September 1946, 'N' class Moguls Nos 1817 and 1854 were painted in Bulleid's Malachite Green livery with black edging and yellow lining. The green was applied in the style adopted by Ashford in 1938. Boiler, cab side and front, tender side and rear, running plate valance, footstep backing plates,

Below: 'W' class 2-6-4T No 31921 *circa* 1949. The snifting valves have been removed. The word SOUTHERN and the British Railways number are in Bulleid-style green-shaded characters. The photograph clearly shows the internal line in the SOUTHERN lettering but not in the numerals. *Ian Allan Library*

Above: 'W' class 2-6-4T No 31924 near Hither Green on a freight from Old Oak Common to Hither Green, September 1948. No 31924 has BRITISH RAILWAYS lettering in Bulleid-style characters and the number in Bulleid numerals on both buffer beam and bunker. The snifting valves remain. The train carries mainly general merchandise in sheeted open wagons or vans. *P. Ransome Wallis*

cylinder cladding and wheels were green. The smoke deflectors were black.

With the Bulleid-style lettering, the running number was applied to the cabside in place of the numberplate, and the word SOUTHERN was placed centrally on the tender or tank side. The sans serif block letters were gilt, with a fine body colour line inside the letters. Numerals were shaded black and did not have the body coloured inside line. The gilt was later changed to golden yellow. In 1941, the lettering was changed to the 'Sunshine' style. Both the numerals and the word SOUTHERN were now shaded, gilt characters with black shading on green locomotives and golden yellow characters with green shading on black locomotives.

Below: 'N' class No 31833 approaching St Kew Highway on a down north Cornwall line freight *circa* 1950. Livery is now BR-lined black with the cabside numerals and BRITISH RAILWAYS title in cream Gill Sans characters. *B. A. Butt*

British Railways liveries

From February to October 1948, the unlined black livery was continued but with BRITISH RAILWAYS lettering, in Bulleid-style characters, on the tender or tanks. A number of locomotives received s-prefixes to the Southern numbers in February and March 1948:

'N' class Nos s1405, s1813, s1814, s1825, s1832, s1838, s1858 and s1871

'U' class Nos s1620 and s1631, 'U1' class s1891 and s1901.

Above: 'U' class No 31627, newly painted in British Railways lined mixed traffic livery. This was carried by all the Moguls, but not the 'W' class, from mid-1949 onwards. Pending availability of transfers for the first BR totem, tenders were unlettered. The cabside number, in cream Gill Sans numerals, is aligned to the centre of the tender panel. A shedplate is yet to be fitted. *Ian Allan Library*

Below: 'N1' class No 31880 at St Leonards, October 1949. Livery is British Railways lined black with an unlettered tender. No shedplate is fitted. *Peter Winding*

Above: 'N' class No 31400 at Ashford, 3 October 1945. This is the usual application of the BR mixed traffic black livery, with cab side numerals and the small first totem. The 4,000gal tender is lined with a rectangular panel on the flat part of the tender. The cab side number is aligned to the totem. *D. L. Bradley*

Below: 'U' class No 31624 passing Worting Junction, probably on the 10.27 (Saturdays) Waterloo–Andover Junction, 21 July 1951. No 31624 has lined black livery with the large first totem and Guildford shedplate. The very mixed train formation is led by a 1918-built LSWR corridor brake composite, a lavatory third from one of the 1906 four-car sets and an earlier LSWR non-corridor carriage rebuilt on an SR underframe. *E. D. Bruton*

Unlined black with British Railways numerals and BRITISH RAILWAYS lettering was applied between March and October 1948 to:
'N' class Nos 31400, 31401, 31404, 31810, 31818, 31839, 31840, 31846, 31857, 31869, 31873 and 31874
'U' class Nos 31610, 31612, 31616, 31634, 31636, 31800, 31801 and 31802
'U1' class Nos 31892, 31897, 31908 and 31910.

Additionally, a number of locomotives had the British Railways numbers applied to their existing Southern livery.

From October 1948, red, grey and cream lining to LNWR style was applied to all the Moguls but the 'W'

Top: 'U' class No 31637 at Ashford in the early 1950s. In this case, the cab side numerals do not line up with the totem on the tender. *D. L. Bradley*

Above: 'W' class No 31923 in unlined black with the small first BR totem at Hither Green, 4 March 1957. The 'Ws' were originally built with flat-topped domes but No 31923 now has a rounded dome. *G. Wheeler*

Right: 'U' class No 31621 with new frames and cylinders but retaining a Maunsell chimney. This view shows the usual arrangement of cab side lining and the 4P3F power classification. *P. Ransome Wallis*

class remained unlined. With this livery, four varieties of tender or tankside lettering were carried in the following order:

- BRITISH RAILWAYS lettering in Gill Sans characters
- Unlettered from late 1948
- British Railways first 'lion on wheel' totem from late 1949
- British Railways second 'lion carrying wheel' totem from mid-1957

Above: 'U' class No 31639, with original cylinders and BR Class 4 chimney, awaiting the arrival of the RCTS 'Solent Railtour' at Fareham, 20 March 1966. No 31639 is fitted with AWS and carries electrification warning flashes. Note the water treatment yellow triangle on the cabside. *Ian Allan Library*

Below: 'W' class No 31921 in unlined black with the second BR totem at Norwood, 16 July 1961. It now carries the power classification 6F above the number, and electrification warning flashes on the front footsteps, tank front and firebox sides. *A. G. Coombs*

The lion in the first totem always faced forwards on both sides of the locomotive. The second emblem was the 'crest' of the coat of arms of the British Transport Commission (BTC), formally approved by the Royal College of Arms (RCA). At first, left-hand and right-hand versions were produced, facing forward on both sides of the locomotive. After the RCA pointed out that only the left-facing lion had been approved, a left-facing lion was applied on both sides from late 1958.

Smokebox numberplates were fitted during works repairs from around September 1948, and shedplates from around August 1950. Shedplates were fitted at running sheds as well as at main works. Although the western section of the Southern Railway had used power classifications for locomotives, these were used only on locomotives allocated to Eastleigh for maintenance and had never been applied to any of the Moguls. British Railways adopted the power classification system used by the LMSR. In 1952, the 2-6-0s were all classified '4MT' and the 'W' 2-6-4Ts as 5F but the classification did not appear on the locomotives. In 1954, the classifications were altered to 4P5F for classes 'N' and 'N1', '4P3F' for classes 'U' and 'U1', and '6F' for the 'W' class. The power

classification was painted on the cab side, above the number, from around 1955.

Yellow discs were painted on the cab sides below the number on locomotives fitted with the British Railways water treatment system in the mid-1950s. The circle was later replaced by a triangle, to avoid confusion with the Western Region's route coding discs. From the late 1950s, electrification warning plates were added to many of the Moguls. These were white with a red lightning flash and were fixed near the front edge of each smoke deflector plate, to either side of the firebox, near the top and on the rear of the tender, below the top lamp bracket. On the 'Ws', these were on the front footsteps, the front face of the tanks and the rear of the bunker.

Below: 'N' class No 31863 stands in Ashford, Kent, station awaiting for the signal to clear before proceeding to the motive power depot in March 1961. *B. E. Coates*

CHAPTER EIGHT

Allocation and Use

The Maunsell Moguls, in particular the 'N' class,
were the nearest the Southern Railway got to a
'goes anywhere' locomotive. The 2-6-4T and the three-cylinder
locomotives were more restricted in their operation.

The 'N' class 2-6-0s

The 'N' class 2-6-0s could be found in most parts of the
SR system, from Ramsgate to Padstow. They could run
over most main and secondary lines, but were restricted
by width from the Tonbridge to Hastings line and by
weight from some smaller branch lines. The prototype 'N'
class, SE&CR No 810, was based at Bricklayers Arms in
south London and was used on mainline freight traffic on
the ex-SER main lines. The Ashford-built locomotives
Nos 811-824 and A825 were also allocated to the ex-SER
main lines, but could also run over the LCDR lines after
these were upgraded in early SR days.

When the Woolwich-built locomotives came into
service, Nos A826-A860 were sent to the West Country,
mainly to Exmouth Junction (Exeter) but three went to
Salisbury and four to Barnstaple. The Urie/Maunsell
4-6-0s of classes 'H15', 'N15' and 'S15' were not
permitted to work west of Exeter and the Moguls took over
most of the freight and some of the passenger traffic on
the lines from Exeter to Plymouth, north Devon and north
Cornwall. Nos A861-A875 joined the ex-SE&CR
locomotives on the eastern section, being allocated to the
ex-LCDR Battersea shed, later known as Stewarts Lane, as
well as to Bricklayers Arms, Redhill, Ashford and Dover.
The final Ashford-built locomotives Nos 1400-1414 were
divided between eastern and western sections.

During the 1920s and early 1930s, the 'Ns' were all
either at the eastern or western ends of the Southern
Railway. The western section locomotives were all west

of Salisbury and no 'N' class 2-6-0s were allocated to the
Central section initially, although Eastern section
locomotives ran over central section lines on specials. The
central section had its own 'K' class 2-6-0s for similar
work. From 1932, a few 'Ns' were based at New Cross
Gate, Eastbourne and Norwood Junction. By 1945, 'Ns'
were also allocated to Reading and Eastleigh. Following
electrification of the Kent main lines in 1959-61 'Ns' were
also allocated to Brighton, Guildford and Weymouth.

Twenty-three 'N' class locomotives were transferred
to the Western Region with the Southern lines west of
Salisbury at the end of 1962 but continued to work on the
ex-SR lines, although being progressively replaced by
Western Region diesels and multiple-units. The 'Ns' were
withdrawn from service between November 1962 and
June 1966.

The 'K' class 2-6-4Ts and 'U' class 2-6-0s

The prototype 'K' class 2-6-4T No 790 was allocated
initially to Bricklayers Arms and worked mainly on
passenger trains between London and Folkestone via
Sevenoaks or Redhill. By 1926, the 'River' class were
allocated to Eastbourne (Nos A795-A799), Redhill (Nos
A790-A794, A808), Dover (Nos A800-A804) and Reading
(Nos A805-A807). All worked passenger trains over the
main lines from London to Brighton, Eastbourne and
Dover, and over the Reading to Redhill line.

After rebuilding as 2-6-0s, the 'Us' were allocated to
Eastbourne, Redhill, Reading, Guildford and Nine Elms,

continuing to work passenger services from London to Brighton and Eastbourne, including the route via East Grinstead, and Reading to Redhill. The western section 'Us' worked secondary passenger services to Portsmouth, Southampton and Salisbury. The 'Us' therefore appeared widely on those parts of the Southern where the 'Ns' were largely absent. After electrification of the Brighton and Eastbourne lines, 'Us' were allocated to Dover, Ashford, Bournemouth and Yeovil, mainly for secondary passenger work but also on freight work. By 1945, three were at Exmouth Junction so the 'Us' really could appear anywhere on the Southern system. By 1955, except for three at Redhill, all were on the western section, none further west than Yeovil. Seven were transferred to the Western Region at the end of 1962 and all were withdrawn between November 1962 and June 1966.

Above: 'N' class No 31410 leaving Herne Bay on a Ramsgate–Victoria express, July 1956. A feature unique on this locomotive was the additional plates to the top of the smoke deflectors. The train appears to consist entirely of BR standard carriages in carmine and cream, led by four-car set No 869. *P. Ransome Wallis*

Above right: SE&CR 'N' class No 813 heading a freight train with an unusually high proportion of vans, circa 1920. The 'N' class was designed with freight work as a prime function on the SE&CR. *Ian Allan Library*

Centre right: Woolwich built 'N' class A852 on freight at an unidentified location. No A852 is fitted with a mechanical lubricator above the left cylinder. This was carried until withdrawal, although it was moved further back when smoke deflectors were fitted. *Ian Allan Library*

Right: 'N' class near Teynham on a London Bridge to Ramsgate train, via the Chiselhurst loop and Chatham. The long formation of ex SE&CR non-corridor carriages and the train reporting number suggest that this is a holiday extra train. *Ian Allan Library*

Above: 'N' class No 1414 approaching Grateley, between
Salisbury and Andover, on an up stopping train in the 1930s.
The train comprises a four-car set of ex-LSWR timber
framed vehicles, but with an ex-LBSCR brake third on the
rear. These carriages were all withdrawn or rebuilt onto new
steel frames in 1935/7. The third track is the Bulford branch,
which ran alongside the main line west of Grateley before
diverging. *Author's collection*

Below: 'N' class No 31407 heads the up Saturday 'Kentish
Belle' Pullman near Herne Bay in the 1950s. No 31407 has
smoke deflectors with a vertical grab rail and two handholes
in the front edge. *P. Ransome Wallis*

Above: SE&CR 'K' class No 790 passing Honor Oak Park (LBSCR) on a train of Great Eastern Railway horseboxes, possibly conveying racehorses from Newmarket to Epsom, *circa* 1920. *Author's collection*

Below: 'K' class No A802 *River Cuckmere* heading a mixed bag of ex-LC&DR and SER carriages with an LSWR third on the front. It appears to be on a 'Special', the headcode suggests Victoria to Crystal Palace. *Author's collection*

Above: 'U' class No 31628 piloting No 35018 *British India Line* past Ropley on the down 'Bournemouth Belle', 8 January 1961. A bank slip near Winchfield had closed the main line, requiring trains to run via Alton. Both carry the Waterloo to Southampton via Alton headcode. No 31628 has new frames and cylinders, a Maunsell chimney and warning flashes. *J. C. Haydon*

Below: 'U' class No 31628 piloting No 35011 *General Steam Navigation* on the diverted down 'Bournemouth Belle' in the early 1960s. The train has just crossed the A31 road on the approach to Alresford on what is now the Mid-Hants Railway. *Colour-Rail (BRS413)*

Above: 'U' class A633 heading the Brighton to Victoria 'Southern Belle' Pullman near Hassocks *circa* 1931. No A633 was built at Ashford in March, 1931. The line was electrified during 1932. Only vacuum braking is now provided and the six Pullman cars are typically varied. The leading brake coach was built in 1922 on the underframe of an ambulance coach. The second is a 12-wheel car from the early 1920s. The third is a newer eight-wheeled car. The fourth is an original 1908 'Southern Belle' car. Note tha this is higher than the others. *Author's collection*

Below: 'U' class No 31617 passing Tunnel Junction, Salisbury, on a down train on the west of England main line, September 1955. The uniform set of ex-LSWR timber-bodied corridor carriages looks recently overhauled, but has not more than two years to run. The photograph was taken from the bridge carrying the A30 main road over the Salisbury–Southampton line. *Colour-Rail (BRS838)*

Above: 'U' class No 31632 double-heading the first ex-LMS diesel-electric locomotive No 10000 on an up train, leaving Wareham on 5 September 1953. In May 1953, the two LMR mainline diesels joined the three Southern types at Nine Elms, before all five were sent to the LMR in 1955. The train is probably the 1.25pm Weymouth to Waterloo which was diagrammed for a diesel. It is unusually long for Weymouth, with five carriages added to the rear of a six-car dining set, but it is a Saturday. Diesels did not run efficiently when ingesting the exhaust of a steam locomotive. A later BR instruction required the diesel to lead when double-heading. *R. K. Blencowe / B. Knowlman*

Right: 'U' class No 31615 near Sturt Lane Junction on an up train, 10 September 1960. No 31615 has new frames and cylinders and AWS. Guildford duty number 162 included the Saturday-only 1.08pm Andover Junction to Waterloo. The 12-car train formation is clearly a multi-portioned West of England express. *The late Derek Cross*

Right: 'U' class No 31791, with new frames and cylinders, BR Standard Class 4 chimney and AWS, at Shepherdswell on a weedkilling train, April 1960. Shepherdswell was the junction for some of the Kent collieries. The Dover main line via Chatham had been electrified in 1959 and, for safety, the power supply to the sidings was provided by overhead wire. *The late Derek Cross*

'K1' class 2-6-4T and 'U1' three-cylinder 2-6-0s

The 'K1' class three-cylinder 2-6-4T, No A890, was allocated to Bricklayers Arms for Charing Cross to Dover express service and returned there after conversion to a 2-6-0, moving to Battersea in 1929. 'U1' class 2-6-0s A891-A900 were allocated new to Fratton (Portsmouth), working expresses to Waterloo. Nos 1901-1910 were allocated new to Eastbourne, St Leonards (No 1903) and Exmouth Junction (Nos 1905-1910) but all were at Eastbourne by late 1931. In 1933, the Eastbourne 'U1s' were displaced by electrification to Battersea, where they worked Kent coast passenger trains. Battersea also received the ex-Fratton 'U1s' in 1935 except for Nos 1894 and 1895 (to Feltham) and No 1898 (to Basingstoke). Between 1937 and 1939, Nos 1890-1892 were at Nine Elms for Reading line services, Nos 1893, 1894, 1895, 1888 and 1899 at Exmouth Junction, and the rest at Battersea. In 1939, Nos 1890 to 1899 moved to Guildford, then in 1942 to Redhill and Reading (Nos 1898/1899).

By 1948, Nos 1890-1900 were on the Central section, Nos 1895-1899 at Redhill, the others at Brighton, working to London via Uckfield and other passenger services on non-electrified lines, whilst Nos 1901-1910 were on the Eastern section. In 1952-4, Nos 31907-31910 were at Nine Elms on various special train and freight work, including the summer Saturday Waterloo to Lymington Pier trains as far as Brockenhurst, where they would fit on the turntable. By 1955, all were on the eastern section but were dispersed by the Kent coast electrification to various duties on the central and western sections. All were withdrawn between November 1962 and July 1963.

'N1' class three-cylinder 2-6-0s

No 822 was allocated new to Bricklayers Arms for mainline goods work with some secondary passenger work. Nos A876-A880 went new to New Cross Gate for central section mainline freight work. Nos 1878-1880 were briefly at Eastbourne during 1935 but all were subsequently on the eastern section at Tonbridge or Bricklayers Arms. The duties of the Tonbridge 'N1s' included freight and some passenger work on the Hastings line. In 1946, Nos 1822, 1876 and 1877 were at Tonbridge and Nos 1878-80 at Hither Green, where all ended up by 1950, returning to Tonbridge with the Kent coast electrification in 1959. All were withdrawn in November 1962.

Below: on 14 January 1961 'U1' class No 31907 is seen on shed at Tonbridge. *Colour-Rail (340106)*

Above: 'U1' class No 1907 approaching Southerham Junction, east of Lewes, on a Victoria to Eastbourne express in the early 1930s. *O. J. Morris*

Below: 'U1' class No 1899 approaching Alton on a Waterloo–Southampton train. Although not dated, the year can be placed around 1936. The ex-LSWR four-car set has been reduced to three cars and the timber-framed carriage (centre) has been rebuilt onto a standard SR underframe. Three-car sets were SE&CR practice and the western section have pointedly added an ex-SER carriage to make the set up to four again. The Woking to Alton line was electrified in July 1937. *Lens of Sutton collection*

'W' class 2-6-4Ts

Until their final years, the 'W' class 2-6-4Ts were all based in the London area for working cross-London freight trains from the railways north of the Thames. They worked occasional empty stock trains but not passenger trains. With the introduction of the 'Crompton' Type 3 diesel, Nos 31923 and 31924 moved to Feltham for freight and empty stock workings. In 1961, Nos 31911, 31913, 31916 and 31922 were transferred to Eastleigh to work oil trains between the Fawley refinery and Eastleigh. In 1962, Nos 31911, 31912, 31913, 31914, 31916, 31917 and 31924 were transferred to Exmouth Junction for local freight work and for banking between Exeter St Davids and Central stations. All were withdrawn between February 1963 and August 1964.

Above: 'U1' class No 1894 heading a train of LNER Gresley carriages in the mid-1940s. No 1894 is in Bulleid's black livery and has a wartime blackout curtain on the front of the tender. The photograph has no caption but the location appears to be the East Coast main line, north of Peterborough, with the LMS Leicester line to the right. It is possible that the train is carrying troops but, once off the Southern, the headcode shows only that it is a class 1 express passenger train. *Author's collection*

Below: 'W' class No 31913 passing Streatham Hill carriage sidings with a Battersea to Norwood freight, 9 April 1963. *S. Creer*

'N' Class Allocations

Loco	1925	1939	1948	1959	Loco	1925	1939	1948	1959
1400		Ashford	Ashford	Ashford	1836	Exmouth Jn	Exmouth Jn	Exmouth Jn	Exmouth Jn
1401		Ashford	Ashford	Ashford	1837	Exmouth Jn	Exmouth Jn	Exmouth Jn	Exmouth Jn
1402		Ashford	Ashford	Ashford	1838	Exmouth Jn	Exmouth Jn	Exmouth Jn	Exmouth Jn
1403		Ashford	Ashford	Ashford	1839	Barnstaple	Exmouth Jn	Exmouth Jn	Exmouth Jn
1404		Ashford	Ashford	Ashford	1840	Exmouth Jn	Barnstaple	Exmouth Jn	Exmouth Jn
1405		Ashford	Battersea	Ashford	1841	Barnstaple	Exmouth Jn	Exmouth Jn	Exmouth Jn
1406		Exmouth Jn	Redhill	Ashford	1842	Exmouth Jn	Exmouth Jn	Exmouth Jn	Exmouth Jn
1407		Exmouth Jn	Exmouth Jn	Ashford	1843	Exmouth Jn	Exmouth Jn	Redhill	Exmouth Jn
1408		Exmouth Jn	Exmouth Jn	Battersea	1844	Exmouth Jn	Exmouth Jn	Norwood Jn	Exmouth Jn
1409		Exmouth Jn	Exmouth Jn	Battersea	1845	Salisbury	Okehampton	Exmouth Jn	Exmouth Jn
1410		Brick Arms	Battersea	Battersea	1846	Exmouth Jn	Exmouth Jn	Salisbury	Exmouth Jn
1411		Brick Arms	Battersea	Battersea	1847	Exmouth Jn	Exmouth Jn	Exmouth Jn	Exmouth Jn
1412		Brick Arms	Battersea	Battersea	1848	Exmouth Jn	Barnstaple	Salisbury	Ashford
1413		Salisbury	Battersea	Battersea	1849	Barnstaple	Okehampton	Redhill	Exmouth Jn
1414		Salisbury	Battersea	Battersea	1850	Exmouth Jn	Salisbury	Reading	Faversham
1810	Brick Arms	Battersea	Battersea	Battersea	1851	Salisbury	Salisbury	Redhill	Brick Arms
1811	Brick Arms	Battersea	Battersea	Battersea	1852	Exmouth Jn	Exmouth Jn	Redhill	Faversham
1812	Ashford	Battersea	Battersea	Battersea	1853	Exmouth Jn	Exmouth Jn	Exmouth Jn	Brick Arms
1813	Brick Arms	Eastbourne	Battersea	Salisbury	1854	Exmouth Jn	Exmouth Jn	Reading	Ashford
1814	Brick Arms	Eastbourne	Norwood Jn	Salisbury	1855	Exmouth Jn	Exmouth Jn	Exmouth Jn	Hither Green
1815	Battersea	Eastbourne	Redhill	Gillingham	1856	Exmouth Jn	Exmouth Jn	Exmouth Jn	Hither Green
1816	Brick Arms	New + Gate	Redhill	Gillingham	1857	Barnstaple	Exmouth Jn	Reading	Hither Green
1817	Brick Arms	Brick Arms	Redhill	Redhill	1858	Exmouth Jn	Exmouth Jn	Redhill	Hither Green
1818	Ashford	Brick Arms	Redhill	Dover	1859	Exmouth Jn	Exmouth Jn	Tonbridge	Hither Green
1819	Dover	Brick Arms	Dover	Dover	1860	Exmouth Jn	Exmouth Jn	Reading	Hither Green
1820	Battersea	Brick Arms	Dover	Dover	1861	Redhill	Brick Arms	Reading	Hither Green
1821	Brick Arms	Brick Arms	Dover	Dover	1862	Battersea	Brick Arms	Tonbridge	Redhill
1823	Battersea	Ashford	Dover	Brick Arms	1863	Battersea	Brick Arms	Redhill	Redhill
1824	Brick Arms	Ashford	Brick Arms	Brick Arms	1864	Redhill	Brick Arms	Redhill	Redhill
1825	Brick Arms	Ashford	Brick Arms	Brick Arms	1865	Brick Arms	Dover	Brick Arms	Redhill
1826	Exmouth Jn	Exmouth Jn	Brick Arms	Brick Arms	1866	Battersea	Dover	Eastleigh	Redhill
1827	Exmouth Jn	Exmouth Jn	Eastleigh	Brick Arms	1867	Battersea	Dover	Eastleigh	Redhill
1828	Exmouth Jn	Exmouth Jn	Exmouth Jn	Brick Arms	1868	Battersea	Dover	Reading	Redhill
1829	Exmouth Jn	Exmouth Jn	Eastleigh	Brick Arms	1869	Battersea	New + Gate	Exmouth Jn	Redhill
1830	Exmouth Jn	Barnstaple	Tonbridge	Exmouth Jn	1870	Battersea	New + Gate	Eastleigh	Brick Arms
1831	Exmouth Jn	Exmouth Jn	Fratton	Exmouth Jn	1871	Brick Arms	Brick Arms	Exmouth Jn	Brick Arms
1832	Exmouth Jn	Exmouth Jn	Exmouth Jn	Exmouth Jn	1872	Brick Arms	Brick Arms	Salisbury	Brick Arms
1833	Exmouth Jn	Barnstaple	Exmouth Jn	Exmouth Jn	1873	Brick Arms	Brick Arms	Salisbury	Brick Arms
1834	Salisbury	Exmouth Jn	Exmouth Jn	Exmouth Jn	1874	Brick Arms	Brick Arms	Exmouth Jn	Brick Arms
1835	Exmouth Jn	Barnstaple	Exmouth Jn	Exmouth Jn	1875	Battersea	Brick Arms	Exmouth Jn	Brick Arms

Brick Arms = Bricklayers Arms   New + Gate = New Cross Gate

'U' Class Allocations

Loco No	1931	1935	1948	1959	Loco No	1921	1935	1948	1959
1610	Guildford	Guildford	Reading	Yeovil	1635	Redhill	Dover	Exmouth Jn	Guildford
1611	Guildford	Guildford	Reading	Eastleigh	1636	Redhill	Redhill	Salisbury	Guildford
1612	Guildford	Guildford	Salisbury	Guildford	1637	Redhill	Redhill	Nine Elms	Fratton
1613	Guildford	Guildford	Nine Elms	Eastleigh	1638	Redhill	Guildford	Exmouth Jn	Fratton
1614	Guildford	Guildford	Guildford	Bournemouth	1639	Redhill	Guildford	Faversham	Guildford
1615	Guildford	Guildford	Reading	Bournemouth	1790	Eastbourne	Yeovil	Yeovil	Exmouth Jn
1616	Guildford	Guildford	Nine Elms	Guildford	1791	Eastbourne	Yeovil	Yeovil	Exmouth Jn
1617	Guildford	Guildford	Nine Elms	Nine Elms	1792	Eastbourne	Yeovil	Yeovil	Eastleigh
1618	Guildford	Guildford	Salisbury	Eastleigh	1793	Eastbourne	Yeovil	Yeovil	Eastleigh
1619	Guildford	Guildford	Nine Elms	Eastleigh	1794	Eastbourne	Yeovil	Yeovil	Eastleigh
1620	Guildford	Guildford	Reading	Eastleigh	1795	Eastbourne	Yeovil	Yeovil	Eastleigh
1621	Guildford	Guildford	Guildford	Nine Elms	1796	Eastbourne	Guildford	Bournemouth	Eastleigh
1622	Guildford	Guildford	Bournemouth	Guildford	1797	Eastbourne	Guildford	Fratton	Guildford
1623	Guildford	Guildford	Guildford	Yeovil	1798	Eastbourne	Guildford	Guildford	Guildford
1624	Guildford	Guildford	Bournemouth	Nine Elms	1799	Eastbourne	Guildford	Guildford	Guildford
1625	Nine Elms	Guildford	Exmouth Jn	Guildford	1800	Redhill	Ashford	Guildford	Guildford
1626	Eastbourne	Nine Elms	Salisbury	Exmouth Jn	1801	Reading	Ashford	Guildford	Eastleigh
1627	Eastbourne	Bournemouth	Basingstoke	Guildford	1802	Reading	Redhill	Guildford	Eastleigh
1628	Eastbourne	Bournemouth	Reading	Guildford	1803	Reading	Redhill	Guildford	Eastleigh
1629	Eastbourne	Bournemouth	Basingstoke	Eastleigh	1804	Redhill	Ashford	Guildford	Fratton
1630	Battersea	Dover	Salisbury	Guildford	1805	Nine Elms	Nine Elms	Guildford	Fratton
1631	Battersea	Dover	Faversham	Guildford	1806	Nine Elms	Nine Elms	Guildford	Basingstoke
1632	Battersea	Basingstoke	Basingstoke	Bournemouth	1807	Nine Elms	Nine Elms	Reading	Fratton
1633	Battersea	Dover	Basingstoke	Eastleigh	1808	Nine Elms	Nine Elms	Faversham	Fratton
1634	Battersea	Dover	Basingstoke	Guildford	1809	Nine Elms	Nine Elms	Guildford	Fratton

'U1' Class Allocations

Loco No	1931	1939	1948	1959	Loco No	1931	1939	1948	1959
1890	Battersea	Guildford	Brighton	Brick Arms	1901	Eastbourne	Battersea	Brick Arms	Brick Arms
1891	Fratton	Exmouth Jn	Brighton	Brick Arms	1902	Eastbourne	Battersea	Brick Arms	Brick Arms
1892	Fratton	Exmouth Jn	Brighton	Faversham	1903	Eastbourne	Battersea	Battersea	Faversham
1893	Fratton	Exmouth Jn	Brighton	Faversham	1904	Eastbourne	Battersea	Battersea	Stewarts Ln
1894	Fratton	Exmouth Jn	Brighion	Stewarts Ln	1905	Eastbourne	Battersea	Battersea	Stewarts Ln
1895	Fratton	Exmouth Jn	Redhill	Stewarts Ln	1906	Eastbourne	Battersea	Battersea	Stewarts Ln
1896	Fratton	Exmouth Jn	Redhill	Tonbridge	1907	Eastbourne	Battersea	Battersea	Stewarts Ln
1897	Fratton	Exmouth Jn	Redhill	Stewarts Ln	1908	Eastbourne	Battersea	Battersea	Tonbridge
1898	Fratton	Exmouth Jn	Redhill	Stewarts Ln	1909	Eastbourne	Battersea	Battersea	Tonbridge
1899	Fratton	Guildford	Redhill	Brick Arms	1910	Eastbourne	Battersea	Battersea	Tonbridge
1900	Eastbourne	Battersea	Brighton	Brick Arms					

'N1' Class Allocations

Loco No	1931	1939	1948	1959	Loco No	1931	1939	1948	1959
1822	Brick Arms	Tonbridge	Battersea	Hither Green	1878	New + Gate	Brick Arms	Hither Green	Hither Green
1876	New + Gate	Brick Arms	Battersea	Hither Green	1879	New + Gate	Tonbridge	Hither Green	Hither Green
1877	New + Gate	Brick Arms	Battersea	Hither Green	1880	New + Gate	Tonbridge	Hither Green	Hither Green

'W' Class Allocations

Loco No	1939	1948	1955	1963	Loco No	1939	1948	1955	1963
1911	Battersea	Hither Green	Hither Green	Exmouth Jn	1919	Norwood Jn	Norwood Jn	Hither Green	Norwood Jn
1912	Battersea	Battersea	Hither Green	Exmouth Jn	1920	Norwood Jn	Norwood Jn	Hither Green	Norwood Jn
1913	Battersea	Hither Green	Hither Green	Norwood Jn	1921	Hither Green	Hither Green	Stewarts Ln	Norwood Jn
1914	Battersea	Battersea	Stewarts Ln	Exmouth Jn	1922	Hither Green	Hither Green	Hither Green	Feltham
1915	Battersea	Battersea	Stewarts Ln	Exmouth Jn	1923	Hither Green	Hither Green	Hither Green	
1916	Norwood Jn	Norwood Jn	Hither Green	Exmouth Jn	1924	Hither Green	Hither Green	Hither Green	Exmouth Jn
1917	Norwood Jn	Norwood Jn	Hither Green	Feltham	1925	Hither Green	Hither Green	Hither Green	Norwood Jn
1918	Norwood Jn	Norwood Jn	Hither Green	Norwood Jn					

Below: 'W' class 2-6-4T No 31919 at Sydenham flyover on empty stock from New Cross Gate to Victoria on 26 June 1954. Although never permitted to work passenger trains, empty stock working was allowed. The train is a long set of ex-SE&CR carriages. *S.C.Nash*

Bottom: 'W' class 2-6-4T 31922 passing Eastleigh station with empty Esso oil tanks for Fawley oil refinery on 1 August 1962. These would have been brought to Eastleigh by a '9F' 2-10-0, the 'Ws' being used for the local trip to Fawley. The tanks are black-painted 35ton vacuum-braked Class B type, and two empty vacuum-braked wagons are marshalled between the tanks and the locomotive and the brake van. *Author*

Preservation

Despite their historical significance, a Maunsell Mogul was not included in the list of locomotives to be preserved which was drawn up on behalf of the British Transport Commission in 1960. The survival of five locomotives, one 'N' and four 'Us', is due to them being sold as scrap to Woodham Bros of Barry Docks, South Wales. Between 1959 and 1968, this company purchased over 250 steam locomotives from British Railways for scrap but 213 of them were never cut up, initially due to a fall in the price of scrap but later because the yard's proprietor, Dai Woodham, found that he had other customers to sell to. The developing railway preservation movement took advantage of the continued existence of these locomotives and, in September 1968, Midland Railway '4F' class 0-6-0 No 43924 became the first locomotive to leave Barry for the Keighley & Worth Valley Railway.

The second locomotive to leave Barry was Maunsell 'U' class Mogul No 31618 which was purchased by the Maunsell Locomotive Society. It left Barry in January 1969 for the Kent & East Sussex Railway but moved to the Bluebell Railway in May 1977. It was followed by 'N' class No 31874 in March 1974, which went to the Mid-

Hants Railway and worked the first train on the reopened line in 1977. 'U' class No 31806 went to the Mid-Hants in October 1976, and No 31625 in March 1980. The last Maunsell Mogul remaining at Barry, 'U' class No 31638, went to the Bluebell Railway in July 1980. All five have subsequently been restored and run but only No 31806 is currently in service. The two on the Bluebell did not receive new frames and have been restored to Maunsell livery as Nos 1618 and 1638. The three on the Mid-Hants all had new frames so could only correctly carry British Railways lined black livery which, fortuitously, fits in with the '1960s image' policy of the railway.

Below: 'U' class No 31806 is preserved on the Mid-Hants Railway. It returned to service in 2011 following an overhaul, it is seen here at Alresford in May 1987 after its initial restoration. Built as a 'K' class 2-6-4T at Brighton in 1917 it was named *River Torridge*, and rebuilt in the form we see it today in 1928. The rebuilt 'Rivers' can be distinguished by a lower running plate and deeper splashers. *Derek Wingate*

CHAPTER NINE

The Irish 'Woolwiches'

Parts for the 27 Woolwich Arsenal 'N' class
were purchased by Irish railways and were completed
as 26 broad gauge 2-6-0s in two classes.

The Midland Great Western Railway of Ireland (MGWR) had a main line 126½ miles (203.6km) long, leading straight across the centre of Ireland from Dublin to Galway. From this line, lines led north-west to Westport and Sligo and there were numerous branches. In 1917, the Chief Mechanical Engineer of the MGWR, Walter Morton, recommended the purchase of five 2-6-0s, but large-wheeled 0-6-0s were purchased instead. In 1923, 12 sets of Maunsell 'N' class parts were ordered from Woolwich Arsenal and delivered to the MGWR's Broadstone works in Dublin. The kits of parts were far from complete and only one locomotive, MGWR No 49, had been finished when politics intervened.

In a similar manner to the Grouping of the British railways in 1923, the government of the Irish Free State decreed that all the railway companies operating entirely within the Free State should be amalgamated. The new Great Southern Railways (Ireland) (GSR) came into being on 1 January 1925. The dominant company within the GSR was Maunsell's old company, the Great Southern & Western Railway (GS&WR). The 12 2-6-0s were completed at Broadstone works in 1925/6 but were now GSR Nos 372-383, although MGWR No 49 briefly carried the number No 410. It never ran in traffic either as No 49 or as No 410.

The GSR (ex-GS&WR) Inchicore works in Dublin used an alphanumeric classification for locomotives, similar to that used by the LNER. Both the LNER and GSR used the letter 'K' for 2-6-0s and the Maunsell Moguls became class 'K1', although the running department generally called them the '372' class. In 1925, the GSR purchased a further 15 sets of parts and four spare boilers and assembled Nos 384-391 at Inchicore in 1927-9. Six more, Nos 393-398, were assembled at Inchicore in 1930 but with 6ft (1.83m) driving wheels, classified 'K1a' or the '393' class. The boiler centreline was raised to 8ft 6in (2.60m). The front and rear drops of the platform were altered to give the correct buffer beam and dragbox heights. There was no No 392 and the 27th set of parts, which was probably far from complete, was never built up. In Ireland, they were known as 'Woolwiches'.

As first assembled, the 'Woolwiches' were identical to the original SE&CR design but with the frame components, smokebox saddles and wheelsets modified to suit the Irish 5ft 3in (1.6m) gauge. Buffer beams and platforms were widened but the cab and tender tank were to the original width. The cylinder by-pass valves were fitted only to No 372 and, possibly 373. As with the Southern locomotives, the footsteps on the motion brackets and the piston tailrods disappeared in the 1930s. Of those modifications carried out by the Southern, the Irish locomotives were never fitted with the second vacuum cylinder on the tender, smoke deflectors or front footsteps. The snifting valves were never removed. Other modifications carried out on the Irish locomotives included removal of the doors between the cab and tender,

Above: GSR Class 372 ('K1') No 385 at Inchicore, 1927. The locomotive is as built from the kit of parts. The cylinder by-pass valves are removed. The front of the tender is cut down to give access to the tablet exchange apparatus. The lamp bracket in front of the smokebox will not be used on the GSR. *Stephenson Locomotive Society*

Below: CIÉ Class 388 ('K1') No 388 at Cork Glanmire Road station on the evening Rosslare boat train, April 1956. No 388 has a tablet catcher on the cab side and is now in unlined black, with no 'flying snail' emblem. *T. J. Edgington / Colour-Rail (IR136)*

Above: GSR class 372 ('K1') No 378 at Broadstone, 25 April 1938. The piston tailrods and the top lamp iron have been removed. The livery is unlined dark grey, which had been introduced on the GS&WR at around the same time as Maunsell introduced it on the SE&CR. The number is carried on a cast plate on the cab side, with small GSR letters above, and also by white blocked No 378 in serif numerals on the buffer beam. *W. A. Camwell / Stephenson Locomotive Society*

Above right: GSR Class 372 ('K1') No 389 fitted with Dabeg feedwater heater at Inchicore, 1928. The piston tailrods are retained and a larger diameter chimney is fitted. *Stephenson Locomotive Society*

Below right: CIÉ Class 372 ('K1') at Broadstone in the 1950s. A larger diameter chimney is fitted and has received a GSR-type smokebox door and snifting valves mounted above the cylinders. The footstep on the motion bracket has been removed. The later type of hinged tablet exchange apparatus is fixed to the cab side, obscuring the number. *W. A. Camwell / Stephenson Locomotive Society*

Shed Allocations of the Woolwiches:

Loco No	1930	1938	1954	Loco No	1930	1938	1954
372	Rosslare	Inchicore	Inchicore	385	Cork	Cork	Inchicore
373	Broadstone	Broadstone	Inchicore	386	Inchicore	Cork	Inchicore
374	Broadstone	Broadstone		387	Cork	Cork	Inchicore
375	Broadstone	Broadstone	Inchicore	388	Broadstone	Broadstone	Cork
376	Broadstone	Broadstone	Broadstone	389	Inchicore	Inchicore	Cork
377	Cork	Cork	Broadstone	390	Inchicore	Inchicore	Cork
378	Broadstone	Broadstone	Broadstone	391	Rosslare	Inchicore	Inchicore
379	Broadstone	Broadstone	Broadstone	393		Broadstone	Broadstone
380	Cork	Cork	Cork	394		Broadstone	Cork
381	Broadstone	Broadstone	Broadstone	395		Cork	Broadstone
382	Rosslare	Waterford	Cork	396		Cork	Broadstone
383	Inchicore	Inchicore	Broadstone	397		Cork	Cork
384	Rosslare	Rosslare	Cork	398		Broadstone	Broadstone

removal of the lagging on the firebox backplate and replacement of the smokebox door and chimney by GSR fittings. No 389 ran with a Dabeg feedwater heater on the left-hand platform during the 1930s. As much of their operation was over single lines, tablet exchange gear was fitted. Initially, this took the form of two horns, one facing forward, the other back, on the tender, with the side sheeting at the front of the tender cut down for access.

During the 1950s, hinged tablet exchange arms of the Whitaker pattern were fitted to the cab sides. During 1947/8 all except Nos 373, 380, 383 and 384 were converted to burn oil but reverted back to coal during 1948.

On the MGWR section, the Moguls were used on the Dublin to Galway line. Provision of larger turntables enabled the type to run to Sligo from 1933 and

Claremorris, on the Westport line, from 1941. After Broadstone station closed in 1937, MGWR section trains ran through to Amiens Street and Westland Row (the present Connolly and Pearse stations in Dublin). On the GS&WR section, Moguls ran over the Dublin to Cork mainline, Mallow to Rosslare, Waterford to Limerick, Kildare and Maryborough (now Portlaoise) to Waterford and Mallow to Killarney, extended to Tralee by 1950. The Moguls were used on both passenger and freight work and provided a very useful intermediate size of locomotive between the GSR's small fleet of 4-6-0s, which were restricted to the Dublin to Cork main line, and the ageing 4-4-0s and 0-6-0s which moved most of the traffic in the south of Ireland.

The 'Woolwiches' all passed to Córas Iompair Éireann (CIÉ), which was set up in 1945 to run all public transport in the Irish Republic. CIÉ was nationalised in 1950 and a programme of investment in diesel traction was initiated, under the control of Oliver Bulleid, who had retired from BR's Southern Region. The 'Woolwiches' were amongst the last steam locomotives to remain in service, latterly mainly on freight work, being withdrawn between 1954 and 1961.

MGWR No 49 appeared briefly in black livery with red lining and carrying MGWR lettering and the

Above: CIÉ class 393 ('K1a') No 396 at Broadstone shed, May 1950. The locomotive is painted dark green with light green lining as used in the early 1950s. The cab side numerals and the 'flying snail' totem appear to be in cream. It has been suggested that the 'flying snails' on green-painted locomotives were eau-de-nil. Broadstone station closed in 1937, but the running shed remained open until 1961. *W. H. G. Boot /Colour-Rail (IR288)*

company's armorial device on the tender. It was then repainted in photographic grey, with black lining, with the GSR number 410 on cast-iron plates on the cab sides. All the 'Woolwiches' actually went into traffic in the GSR livery of unlined dark grey, almost black, with no lettering apart from the cast-iron cabside plates, carrying the number with small GSR letters above. These were replaced by painted numerals during 'The Emergency', the Irish euphemism for World War 2. Smokebox numberplates appeared in about 1950. In 1947, the grey was replaced by unlined black with yellow numerals. From 1948, the 'Woolwiches' were painted green, initially dark green with black edging and light green lining, later light green with black edging and white lining. In 1952, No 388 was painted black with red and white lining to the platform valance, and unlined black became standard from 1954.

Above: GSR class 393 ('K1a') No 398, at Kildare with an up express on the Cork to Dublin main line in the 1930s. With 6ft 0in (1.68m) driving wheels, the GSR 393 was similar to the Southern Railway '16xx' series 'U' class but with the longer coupled wheelbase of the 'N' class. The train consists of GS&WR or GSR corridor stock, with a Pullman car. Four of these went to the GSR in 1926. *Ian Allan Library*

Below: CIÉ Class 393 ('K1a') No 393 at Broadstone, 27 April 1951. No 393 now has a GSR-type smokebox door, snifting valves over the cylinders and smokebox numberplate. The footstep on the motion bracket has been removed. The Irish Moguls were never fitted with front footsteps. Livery appears to be dark green, with no 'flying snail' totem. The earlier type of tablet exchange apparatus is mounted on the tender. *T. J. Edgington / Stephenson Locomotive Society*

CHAPTER TEN

Metropolitan 2-6-4Ts

The London-based Metropolitan Railway required locomotives to work mainline freight services and contracted Armstrong Whitworth to assemble six sets of Woolwich Arsenal parts as 2-6-4Ts, which were later transferred to the LNER.

At the Grouping of the British railways in 1923, a number of railways serving the London area were not included. Most of these were the electrically operated passenger railways owned by the Underground Electric Railways Company of London Ltd (the Underground Group). The Metropolitan Railway operated electric passenger services in central London, integrated with those of the Underground's Metropolitan District Railway but it also had a main line to Aylesbury and Verney Junction on the LNWR Bletchley to Oxford line, 50½ miles (81.3km) from Baker Street station in London, with branches to Chesham and Brill. Electrification went only as far as Harrow, but was extended to Rickmansworth in 1925. The Metropolitan had a small fleet of steam locomotives to work passenger trains beyond the limit of electrification. The company also operated commercial freight services over surface lines.

To work the freight services from Verney Junction to Finchley Road, the last station before the mainline went underground, The Metropolitan purchased six sets of Maunsell Mogul parts from Woolwich Arsenal in late 1924 and placed an order with Armstrong Whitworth to assemble them as 2-6-4Ts, using some standard Metropolitan components such as the trailing bogie. The cab had side windows and sliding shutters, and footsteps at both ends of the locomotives were mounted transversely, below the buffer beams. Lamp sockets were used instead of the SE&CR and SR-style lamp irons. The

2-6-4Ts became the 'K' class, coincidentally the same as the Southern 2-6-4Ts, the Irish Moguls and the ex-LBSCR 2-6-0s! All were numbered 111 to 116. The 'Ks' were used mainly on the Verney Junction to Finchley Road freight services but did occasionally work passenger trains north of Rickmansworth. They were not permitted into the tunnel section south of Finchley Road.

In 1933, the London Passenger Transport Board (LPTB) was set up, to operate all passenger transport (apart from that operated by the mainline railway companies) within 30 miles (48km) of London. Metropolitan operations continued unchanged as part of London Transport (LT), even though its outlying operations and freight services were outside the LPTB's remit. Change came in 1937 when LT's new works programme required enlarged electric car sheds at Neasden and the Metropolitan's steam shed was in the way. A new, smaller, shed was built for the locomotives to be retained for works trains whilst the 'G' class 0-6-4Ts, class H 4-4-4Ts and Class K 2-6-4Ts, used on the main line, were transferred to the LNER. By another, numerical, coincidence, they became LNER classes 'M2', 'H2' and 'L2', as the LNER previously had only one class with each of these wheel arrangements. The LNER then worked LT's passenger trains from Rickmansworth to Aylesbury and Chesham and the commercial freight services.

The 'Ks', now LNER 'L2' class Nos 6158-6163, moved to the LNER shed at Neasden and continued to

Above: London Transport No 112 at Amersham on an up freight, June 1938. The side view enables the style of the lining to be clearly seen. Note the balance pipe between the side and back tanks, the sliding shutters to the cab and the hooter, mounted horizontally in front of the cab.
Pendragon collection / Colour-Rail (LT138)

Left: No 111 passing Chorley Wood on an up freight, 2 June 1934. Although now in London Transport ownership, it still carries the Metropolitan title. Note the large numerals on the rear of the bunker with the class letter 'K' below.
H. C. Casserley

Above: Metropolitan No 113 as built. Features unique to these locomotives include the footsteps below the buffer beam, curved handrails over the front drop of the platform, the lamp sockets (five on the buffer beam and one in front of the chimney) and destination board brackets on the front framing. Safety chains are carried on the buffer beam, long after most railways stopped using them. The 'Ks' had mechanical lubricators over the left-hand cylinder, as were fitted to a small number of Southern 'Ns'. *Ian Allan Library*

Right: No 113 in London Transport livery at Neasden. The Metropolitan livery is retained but with LONDON TRANSPORT lettering. A trip cock, which applied the brake if an adverse signal was passed, is mounted under the cylinder. On the opposite side, it was on the bogie. *Ian Allan Library*

Above: Metropolitan No 115 is now LNER 'L2' class No 6162. The only change appears to be the replacement of Metropolitan-style lamp sockets by conventional lamp irons. Livery is now unlined black with shaded yellow lettering and numerals. *Stephenson Locomotive Society*

operate the local freight services, with occasional passenger turns on the Aylesbury trains. For maintenance, they were allocated to the LNER (ex-Great Eastern Railway) Stratford works in east London and gradually began to receive standard LNER fittings such as conventional lamp irons, replacing the sockets. Unlike the SR locomotives, all retained the piston tailrods, snifting valves and the footsteps on the motion brackets throughout service. All were withdrawn from service between 1943

and 1948. Metropolitan Nos 111 and 113 became Nos 9070 and 9071 in the LNER's 1946 renumbering scheme and reached British Railways ownership but never received BR numbers. Nos 9070 and 9071 received LNER standard buffers and No 9071 had a centre dart and handle added to the Maunsell smokebox door.

The Metropolitan livery was maroon with yellow and black lining, METROPOLITAN lettering on the side tanks and cast brass numberplates on the cabside and the rear of the bunker. This livery was continued by LT but with LONDON TRANSPORT lettering. The LNER locomotives were painted unlined black with the number on the tank side and LNER above. In 1941, the lettering became NE but on No 9070 changed to LNER before withdrawal.

Below left: No 116 near Chorley Wood on an Aylesbury train in 1938. The LNER has not yet altered No 116's appearance, apart from the lack of cleaning. Note the collector beam on the bogie of the leading carriage, to provide electric light and heating south of Rickmansworth. *Author's collection*

Below: Metropolitan No 114 is now LNER No 6161, passing the closed Waddesden station, north of Aylesbury, with a freight, 13 May 1939. Metropolitan Line passenger trains stopped running north of Aylesbury in July 1936 but the freights to Verney Junction continued until September 1947. As far as Quainton Road, the line still carried LNER mainline trains to and from Marylebone. *H. C. Casserley*

Above: London Transport No 114 at Amersham in 1938. It is now LNER No 6161 but this is only seen in the deteriorating cleaning standards. *Colour-Rail (LT2)*

Below: Metropolitan No 111 now carries the first LNER number 6158 on the rear buffer beam. The 1946 number 9070 and LNER lettering on the tank side in plain yellow sans serif characters are visible. The rear of the bunker has a complete set of Metropolitan-style lamp and route indicator brackets. The locomotive is standing in the down engine sidings at Rickmansworth on 7 April 1947. *H. C. Casserley*

Appendices

The following tables show the building and withdrawal dates of all the Maunsell Mogul family. The numbers shown are those carried when the locomotives were new and, on all the Southern Railway locomotives, were carried throughout but with letters or figures added by successive owners. Within each table, locomotives are listed in the order in which they were built.

'N' class (2-6-0)
Locomotive Nos 810-822, 824 and A825, and also Nos 1400-1414, were built at Ashford works. Locomotive Nos A826-A875 were built at Woolwich Arsenal and completed at Ashford works, being numbered in the order of entering Ashford for completion. No works numbers were issued by either builder. An (f) against the withdrawal date indicates that the locomotive concerned was fitted with new front or full frames, and a (B) indicates a BR Standard Class 4 chimney was fitted.

No	Date to Service	Withdrawn	No	Date to Service	Withdrawn	No	Date to Service	Withdrawn
810	8/1917	3/1964	A838	7/1924	2/1964 (fB)	A865	6/1925	3/1963 (B)
811	6/1920	7/1965	A839	8/1924	12/1963 (B)	A866	11/1925	1/1966 (B)
812	8/1920	6/1964	A840	8/1924	9/1964 (f)	A867	6/1925	7/1963 (B)
813	9/1920	10/1963	A841	8/1924	3/1964 (B)	A868	7/1925	1/1964 (fB)
814	11/1920	7/1964 (B)	A842	8/1924	9/1965 (fb)	A869	7/1925	8/1964 (fB)
815	12/1920	5/1963 (B)	A843	8/1924	9/1964 (fb)	A870	7/1925	4/1964 (B)
816	12/1921	1/1966	A844	9/1924	12/1963 (B)	A871	7/1925	12/1963 (fB)
817	1/1922	1/1964 (B)	A845	9/1924	9/1964 (fB)	A872	9/1925	5/1963 (B)
818	3/1922	9/1963 (B)	A846	1/1925	9/1964 (f)	A873	9/1925	1/1966 (B)
819	5/1922	1/1964	A847	2/1925	10/1963 (B)	A874	9/1925	3/1964 (fB)
820	8/1922	8/1963	A848	2/1925	2/1964 (f)	A875	8/1925	8/1964 (B)
821	10/1922	5/1964	A849	2/1925	6/1964	1400	7/1932	6/1964 (fB)
823	5/1923	11/1962	A850	2/1925	1/1964	1401	8/1932	7/1965
824	8/1923	9/1963	A851	2/1925	9/1963 (B)	1402	8/1932	8/1963 (B)
A825	12/1923	10/1963 (B)	A852	3/1925	9/1963	1403	8/1932	6/1963
A826	6/1924	9/1963 (B)	A853	4/1925	9/1964 (fB)	1404	10/1932	12/1963
A827	5/1924	9/1963	A854	3/1925	6/1964 (fB)	1405	11/1932	6/1966 (B)
A828	6/1924	6/1964 (B)	A855	3/1925	9/1964 (f)	1406	1/1933	9/1964 (fB)
A829	7/1924	11/1964 (f)	A856	3/1925	9/1964	1407	8/1933	7/1963
A830	6/1924	1/1964 (f)	A857	4/1925	1/1964 (B)	1408	9/1933	6/1966 (fB)
A831	6/1924	4/1965 (fB)	A858	5/1925	12/1965 (fB)	1409	10/1933	11/1962
A832	7/1924	1/1964	A859	4/1925	9/1964	1410	11/1933	11/1964 (B)
A833	7/1924	2/1964 (fB)	A860	4/1925	11/1963	1411	11/1933	4/1966
A834	7/1924	9/1964 (B)	A861	6/1925	5/1963	1412	12/1933	8/1964 (B)
A835	7/1924	9/1964 (fB)	A862	5/1925	4/1965 (fB)	1413	1/1934	6/1964 (fB)
A836	7/1924	12/1963 (B)	A863	5/1925	7/1963 (B)	1414	1/1934	11/1962 (B)
A837	7/1924	9/1964 (fB)	A864	6/1925	1/1964 (fB)			

Southern 'K' and 'K1' class (2-6-4T)

Locomotives Nos 790 and A890 were built at Ashford works, Nos A791-A799 by Armstrong Whitworth & Co from components supplied from Ashford, and Nos A800-A809 at Brighton works. All were withdrawn from service after the Sevenoaks accident in August 1927 and rebuilt as 'U' and 'U1' class 2-6-0s.

No	Name	Works No	Date to Service	No	Name	Works No	Date to Service
790	River Avon *	—	7/1917	A800	River Cray	—	7/1926
A791	River Adur	761	5/1925	A801	River Darenth	—	7/1926
A792	River Arun	762	5/1925	A802	River Cuckmere	—	8/1926
A793	River Ouse	763	5/1925	A803	River Itchen	—	8/1926
A794	River Rother	764	5/1925	A804	River Tamar	—	9/1926
A795	River Medway	765	6/1925	A805	River Camel	—	10/1926
A796	River Stour	766	6/1925	A806	River Torridge	—	10/1926
A797	River Mole	767	6/1925	A807	River Axe	—	11/1926
A798	River Wey	768	6/1925	A808	River Char	—	11/1926
A799	River Test	769	6/1925	A809	River Dart	—	12/1926
				A890**	River Frome	—	12/1925

* No 790 was not named until January 1925, by which time it was A790   ** A890 was the three-cylinder 'K1' class locomotive

'U' class (2-6-0)

Locomotives Nos A790-A796 were rebuilt from 'K' class 2-6-4T at Eastleigh works, Nos A797-A802 and A805 at Ashford, Nos A803, A804 and A806-A809 at Brighton. Nos A610-A629 were built as 2-6-0s at Brighton and Nos A620-A639 at Ashford. An (f) against the withdrawal date indicates that the locomotive had been fitted with new front or full frames, and a (B) indicates that it was fitted with a BR Standard Class 4 chimney.

No	Date to Service	Withdrawn	No	Date to Service	Withdrawn	No	Date to Service	Withdrawn
A790	6/1928	5/1965	A807	6/1928	1/1964 (B)	A624	2/1929	6/1964 (fB)
A791	7/1928	6/1966 (fB)	A808	7/1928	1/1964	A625	3/1929	1/1964 (fB)
A792	7/1928	9/1964 (fB)	A809	7/1928	1/1966 (fB)	A626	3/1929	1/1964
A793	6/1928	5/1964 (B)	A610	8/1928	12/1962	A627	4/1929	10/1965
A794	6/1928	6/1963	A611	8/1928	10/1963 (B)	A628	4/1929	6/1964 (f)
A795	6/1928	6/1963 (fB)	A612	7/1928	5/1963 (B)	A629	12/1929	1/1964 (B)
A796	7/1928	1/1964 (fB)	A613	6/1918	1/1964 (fB)	A630	2/1931	11/1962
A797	7/1928	1/1964	A614	7/1928	11/1963 (fB)	A631	3/1931	9/1963 (f)
A798	8/1928	9/1964	A615	8/1928	10/1963 (fB)	A632	3/1931	9/1964 (B)
A799	7/1928	2/1965 (B)	A616	9/1928	6/1964	A633	3/1931	12/1963 (fB)
A800	12/1928	10/1965 (B)	A617	10/1928	1/1964 (fB)	A634	4/1931	12/1963 (f)
A801	7/1928	6/1964 (B)	A618	10/1928	1/1964 (B)	A635	4/1931	12/1963 (fB)
A802	7/1928	9/1964 (fB)	A619	12/1928	12/1965	A636	4/1931	6/1963
A803	6/1928	3/1966	A620	11/1929	4/1965	A637	5/1931	9/1963 (fB)
A804	6/1928	6/1964 (B)	A621	12/1928	10/1964 (f)	A638	5/1931	1/1964
A805	3/1928	8/1963 (B)	A622	1/1929	1/1964 (fB)	A639	5/1931	6/1966 (B)
A806	6/1928	1/1964 (fB)	A623	1/1929	12/1963 (f)			

'N1' Class (2-6-0)

All were built at Ashford works.

No	Date to Service	Withdrawn	No	Date to Service	Withdrawn	No	Date to Service	Withdrawn
822	3/1923	11/1962	A877	4/1930	11/1962	A879	4/1930	11/1962
A876	3/1930	11/1962	A878	4/1930	11/1962	A880	11/1930	11/1962

'U1' Class (2-6-0)

'U1' class No A890 was rebuilt from the single 'K1' class 2-6-4T at Ashford. Nos A891-A900 and 1901-1910 were built as 2-6-0s at Eastleigh.

No	Date to Service	Withdrawn	No	Date to Service	Withdrawn	No	Date to Service	Withdrawn
A890	6/1928	6/1963	A897	3/1931	11/1962	1904	7/1931	11/1962
A891	1/1931	4/1963	A898	4/1931	12/1962	1905	8/1931	12/1962
A892	1/1931	11/1962	A899	4/1931	12/1962	1906	9/1931	12/1962
A893	2/1931	12/1962	A900	5/1931	12/1962	1907	9/1931	12/1962
A894	2/1931	12/1962	1901	6/1931	6/1963	1908	10/1931	12/1962
A895	3/1931	12/1962	1902	7/1931	11/1962	1909	10/1931	12/1962
A896	3/1931	12/1962	1903	7/1931	12/1962	1910	11/1931	7/1963

'W' Class 2-6-4Ts

Nos 1911-1915 were built at Eastleigh works, and Nos 1916-1925 at Ashford.

No	Date to Service	Withdrawn	No	Date to Service	Withdrawn	No	Date to Service	Withdrawn
1911	1/1932	10/1963	1916	4/1935	7/1963	1921	10/1935	9/1963
1912	1/1932	8/1964	1917	4/1935	1/1964	1922	11/1935	8/1963
1913	1/1932	3/1964	1918	6/1935	8/1963	1923	1/1936	2/1963
1914	1/1932	8/1964	1919	7/1935	11/1963	1924	2/1936	7/1964
1915	2/1932	10/1963	1920	8/1935	7/1963	1925	4/1936	11/1963

Irish 372 and 393 class (2-6-0)

Nos 372-383 were built at Broadstone works, and Nos 384-391 and Nos 393-398 at Inchicore works from parts supplied by Woolwich Arsenal.

No	Date to Service	Withdrawn	No	Date to Service	Withdrawn	No	Date to Service	Withdrawn
372 *	4/1925	11/1960	379	12/1926	10/1959	386	1927	8/1959
373	9/1925	8/1959	380	12/1926	10/1959	387	1928	10/1959
374	11/1925	8/1959	381	12/1926	8/1959	388	1928	9/1962
375 **	2/1926	3/1957	382	1/1927	9/1955	389	1928	3/1955
376	3/1926	10/1961	383	3/1927	10/1959	390	6/1929	6/1955
377	3/1926	2/1960	384	1927	5/1960	391	6/1929	8/1957
378	10/1926	8/1959	385	1927	5/1960			

393 class

No	Date to Service	Withdrawn	No	Date to Service	Withdrawn	No	Date to Service	Withdrawn
393	7/1930	9/1954	395	1930	8/1957	397	1930	11/1957
394	7/1930	10/1959	396	1930	10/1959	398	1930	6/1957

* No 372 was built as MGWR No 49, later GSR 410, but did not run with either number
** No 375 was scrapped where it lay in the River Suir after a runaway at Cahir in 12/1955

Metropolitan 'K' class (2-6-4T)

Built by Armstrong Whitworth & Co incorporating parts supplied by Woolwich Arsenal.

No	Works No	Date to Service	LNER Number	2nd LNER Number	Withdrawn
111	702	3/1925	6158 5/1939	9070 1/1947	10/1948
112	703	3/1925	6159 10/1938	None	1/1943
113	704	3/1925	6160 4/1939	9071 1/1947	10/1948
114	705	3/1925	6161 11/1938	None	5/1943
115	706	3/1925	6162 7/1938	None	1/1946
116	707	3/1925	6163 11/1938	None	5/1945

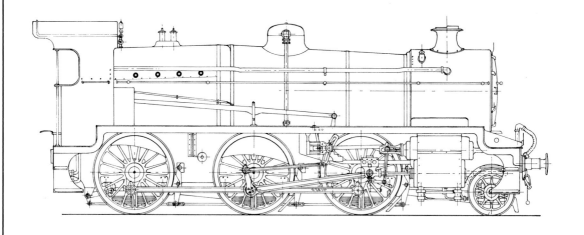

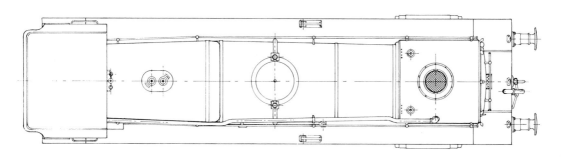

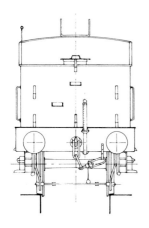

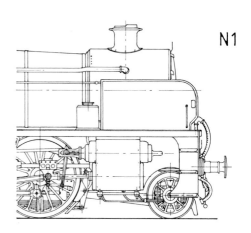

N1

SR Mogul, 'N' and 'N1' class.
© Copyright 2008 Ian Beattie

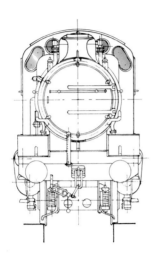
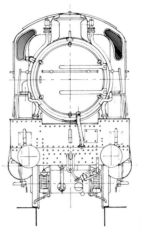

N1

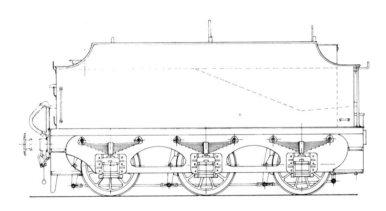

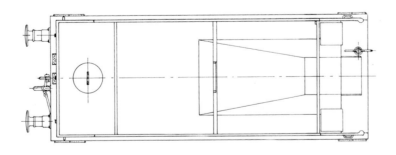

SR Mogul, 'N' and 'N1' class, 'N' class tender.
© Copyright 2008 Ian Beattie

Above: No 1611, a 'U' class 2-6-0 at Guildford on the Margate to Birkenhead through train. The locomotive is painted in Maunsell Dark Green livery but the leading carriage is SR Malachite Green. *Colour-Rail (SR53)*

Below: 'N' No 31853, recently repaired at Ashford, approaching Halwill Junction on a very untypical Padstow train, comprising Eastern Region stock, in August 1960. Behind the maroon GUV is an ex-LNER articulated pair, built in 1935 for East Lincolnshire services, followed by two more LNER carriages, still in crimson and cream. *D. H. Beecroft / Colour-Rail (BRS474)*